Luke Cawley, author of *The Myth of the Non-Christian.*

In *Campus Lights*, it is astonishing how he combines solid knowledge of the world and the Bible with exciting, page-turner storytelling from all corners of the world. The story about IFES is a magnificent story of God at work, about a gospel that knows no country boundaries and about a living Jesus who is not limited by human power structures. Up until now I had thought it almost impossible to grasp and retell the IFES story. Read this book yourself and see if you agree with me that Luke Cawley has made it happen!

Luke is clearly an evangelist. He wants to inspire you to be one too, whether you get your inspiration from the last days of Jesus, from the IFES history or from testimonies about what God is doing among students around the globe today. Get a copy of this one, you want to read it, and you want others to read it too!

TOR ERLING FAGERMOEN
REGIONAL SECRETARY, IFES EUROPE

The history of IFES is a rich tapestry of God's goodness, both then and now. Luke brings to life God's work in IFES today in a thrilling, evocative and engaging manner through stories of students from across the globe. A must read for students and those who love them.

KRISTI MAIR
RESEARCH FELLOW, OAK HILL COLLEGE; AUTHOR OF MORE>TRUTH

I am delighted to commend this book. Luke Cawley invites us to join him on a journey where God inspires his people to small steps of obedience – allowing transformative encounters with Jesus – and through his Holy Spirit leads Christian students around the world to fulfil their part in the Great Commission. A book I will gratefully share with my students.

REVD ZIEL MACHADO
FORMER IFES REGIONAL SECRETARY FOR LATIN AMERICA;
VICE-RECTOR OF SERVANT OF CHRIST THEOLOGICAL SEMINARY,
SÃO PAULO, BRAZIL

A powerful book! Stories from around the world that will leave you at the edge of your seat, encourage you to persevere and share Jesus with boldness wherever he calls.

SARAH BREUEL
REVIVE EUROPE COORDINATOR

i

The growth of IFES around the world may well be the greatest story you have never heard. Generations of student leaders have taken initiative, often at great cost, to see the light of Jesus shine on their campuses. The significance of this in reaching the lost, engaging the university, the forming of character and the development of leaders continues to be immense. Nations are shaped as graduates are salt and light in public life, education, healthcare, business, law, sport, the arts, church, family and community. *Campus Lights* is full of encouraging stories about effective student ministry and its ongoing impact. The insights into how ordinary men and women have stepped out in faith with creativity and boldness are inspirational. IFES continues to break new ground and is actively pioneering new work on every continent.

One of the many things I love about this book is the way each chapter concludes with points for reflection and discussion. My hope and prayer is that this will inform conversation globally and that the light will shine brighter and further in the days ahead. I believe that the best is yet to come in the work and witness of IFES around the world, and that this book is essential reading for all who want to be part of the next chapter of this phenomenal story.

NIGEL POLLOCK
PRESIDENT, INTERVARSITY CANADA, PROGRAMME DIRECTOR;
HEAD COACH, IFES BREAKING NEW GROUND INITIATIVE;
FORMER NATIONAL DIRECTOR, TSCF, NEW ZEALAND;
FORMER DIRECTOR, TRAINING AND DEVELOPMENT, UCCF

A fresh and challenging portrayal of God at work in the student world ... Replete with striking illustrations of the passion and courage of evangelical students (and graduates) from every corner of the globe ... a strong justification of the strategic importance and life-shaping influence of ministry in this key area of life.

LINDSAY BROWN
FORMER GENERAL SECRETARY, IFES

Campus Lights reminds us of the importance of reaching students with the gospel and the impact that Christian students continue to have in their communities long after their student years. We are reminded of how God continues to open doors for the gospel on campuses around the world and how he gives creative and innovative ideas for sharing Jesus with others. By blending reflections from the life and ministry of Jesus into each chapter, themes are helpfully unpacked, and we are left challenged and inspired to pray for, support and engage actively in student ministry.

MATTHEW SKIRTON
UK DIRECTOR, OM

There is something remarkable and significant about Christian students from a variety of backgrounds joining together in vibrant student witness to share the good news of Jesus on campus. In these exciting stories, Luke Cawley recounts some of what God is doing on campuses around the world. I encourage you to read them and be encouraged, challenged and inspired.

BEN CARSWELL
NATIONAL DIRECTOR, TERTIARY STUDENTS CHRISTIAN FELLOWSHIP,
NEW ZEALAND

From Mongolia to the Middle East, in the midst of significant struggles and suffering, we have witnessed the extraordinary growth of Christian student movements worldwide. *Campus Lights* is an eye-opening look at campus ministries around the globe – full of stories designed to inspire you, challenge you, and equip you, as you engage universities in your own contexts.

TOM LIN
PRESIDENT, INTERVARSITY CHRISTIAN FELLOWSHIP/USA

Our own perspective on what God is doing in the student world is often limited to our own country or even campus. Luke Cawley poignantly and beautifully lifts our eyes to what God is doing around the world and builds our faith to pray and work towards stories yet unwritten.

PETER DRAY
HEAD OF CREATIVE EVANGELISM, THE UNIVERSITIES AND COLLEGES
CHRISTIAN FELLOWSHIP, GREAT BRITAIN

LUKE CAWLEY

CAMPUS LIGHTS

STUDENTS LIVING AND SPEAKING
FOR JESUS AROUND THE WORLD

Muddy
Pearl

Published in 2019 by
Muddy Pearl, Edinburgh, Scotland.
www.muddypearl.com
books@muddypearl.com

British Library Cataloguing in Publication Data
A catalogue record for this book is available from the British Library
ISBN 978-1-910012-73-4
Typeset in Minion by Revo Creative Ltd, Lancaster
Printed in Great Britain by Bell & Bain Ltd, Glasgow
Cover design by Revo Creative
Cover illustration by Shin Maeng

To Mike and Kris York,
whose long and faithful investment has been to the benefit
of countless students and staff.

CONTENTS

CHAPTER ONE:
SECRET POLICE

STORIES FROM MY PAST (EURASIA)

The police walked in unannounced. They were dressed entirely in black from their snow-flecked boots to their thick woollen hats. Only their badges, flashing reflected light from the restaurant's ceiling lamps, broke the darkness. They didn't come alone: silence entered with them. It came swiftly and smothered us all. It wasn't a tranquil stillness but one infused with horror. Every intricate inch of our bodies remained fixed from the moment that we each, in swift succession, caught a glimpse of the intruders.

We all stood there wordlessly for almost two minutes waiting to see what would happen. I momentarily glanced towards my translator, stood beside me in the centre of the room, and – like me – still holding a microphone in her hand. Just moments previously I had been giving a presentation about whether we can know anything about God. The atmosphere had been warm. Discussion around the tables had been thoughtful and marked by good humour.

Most of the forty students present were attending such an event for the first time in their lives and were enjoying exploring a new topic. Some had a vague awareness that religious events outside church buildings were prohibited by local laws, but the organizers understood that we could talk publicly about a Christian perspective on cultural and philosophical questions so long as we weren't praying, taking up offerings or making an altar call. Avoid these and, legally, you are not committing a religious act.

It seemed the police understood things differently. One of the officers stepped into the centre of the room and made a loud demand. No one responded. More silence as he looked around at us all. Then he pierced the air with a similarly firm command. I whispered to my translator asking what was being said. She replied, almost inaudibly, that they were asking who had organized the event. Nobody wanted to take responsibility as the consequences didn't look good.

Eventually, though, somebody spoke up and asked what the problem was. The officer replied with a question of his own. Why, he asked, were we talking about God? My translator spoke up very calmly, albeit with a slight underlying tremor, and explained that this event was celebrating the anniversary of the Bible being translated into the local language by a great national poet. It is impossible to celebrate such an event without mention of God.

The officer stood impassively for another minute and said nothing. Then he shouted for everyone to pull out their identification documents. I crept across the room, trying to look as innocuous as one can when one is the main speaker at an apparently illegal event, and rummaged through my bag for something I could show them. Others reached for their wallets and pulled out their national identification cards. The police worked their way methodically around the restaurant tables, taking and carefully scrutinizing one card at a time, and – with some – even scribbling individuals' details on their small notepads.

One of the officers came to me and took my driving licence from my hand. I could see an expression of surprise cross his face as he saw I was British. It was the first emotion any of them had displayed since arriving. He crossed the room to consult with a colleague; they whispered together as they looked down at my card for a few moments before walking back and wordlessly returning it to me. Eventually, after about an hour, some of us were permitted to leave and we stepped outside into the snowy street. The four locals identified as the organizers, one of them my translator, were taken by the police for further interrogation.

As I stood outside the restaurant, still in shock from all that had happened, a student approached me. She asked if I had a moment to share what I would have said in the second half of my presentation if the police hadn't shut down proceedings. A few others crowded round to hear my explanation and she relayed it to them in their language. We stood there talking for about twenty minutes before friends arrived and drove us away.

It was just after midnight – some four hours later – before the police released the event's organizers. By that time the local Christian students had been deluged by innumerable SMS and social media messages requesting to hear more about the Christian faith. Some of those contacting them had been present in the restaurant that evening and others had simply heard about it from friends. Like many locals in this nation, where almost half the population identify as agnostic or atheist, they had no idea of the many restrictions and difficulties experienced by their Christian neighbours. How could they, when they themselves never had cause to test the limits of religious freedom? But now they had discovered our message – so dangerous and forbidden that the police wouldn't let us speak of it to even a small crowd of students. Naturally they wanted to find out more for themselves.

THE ESCALATION

The next morning, nine of us Christians (mainly students) crowded into a small room on the fourth floor of a concrete block of flats. Those who had been at the police station said that criminal charges were likely. All the week's planned outreach events at the restaurant had been cancelled by its owners. But the students were determined to find a way to build on the interest of those who had been messaging them. They planned to spend the afternoon trying to find a church leader willing to let them run some kind of event – anything, even a board game night – to which they could invite these new students that evening.

As they were discussing plans, one of the students walked over to the window and pulled the curtain aside. He peered out through the falling snow for a few moments before turning to inform us that the police van, which had been parked outside since the early hours, was still there. For all we knew, our every word was being listened to by law enforcement officers.

We decided to go ahead and pray. Before we did so, one of the students opened a Bible and read from Romans 8. He encouraged us all that things were not spinning out of control. God takes these situations and works them for the good of those who love him.[1] As I looked around the room, I saw the determined faces of the students and staff; the

---

[1] Romans 8:28.

4

events of the previous night seemed only to have hardened their resolve. The prayers which followed were mainly asking God to keep an open door for connecting with the students. By the time we wrapped up, an hour later, the police van had left and we dispersed to seek out a location to which we could invite the previous night's students.

Later in the day, as we were in deep conversation with a local church leader who wanted to lend us his building, we got word that the city police were no longer pursuing our case. The secret police, feared for their harshness and intolerance towards all who run unauthorized gatherings, were now involved instead. They were asking questions at the restaurant and requisitioning security camera footage from the gathering at the restaurant. Shock crossed the students' faces. Our little group swiftly left the building, piled into a van and headed to the train station to buy tickets for the first available ride out of town. Everybody turned off their phones to avoid being tracked.

On our return from the train station, as we drove along the bumpy, icy streets, several of the students noticed that their phones had all become unusually hot in their pockets. Turning them back on, they discovered that their batteries had been drained. Someone was following our movements via GPS. We all removed the batteries from our phones and the van took a sharp turn. Our driver took us out to a secluded house in the country where we could hide until our locomotive was ready to depart.

As we sat together, eating snacks and drinking tea provided by our host, gallows humour flowed among us. One of the organizers joked about how she'd been wanting more time to read and that maybe prison would be a great place to finally get some peace and quiet. Several students commented that they would bake cakes and bring them to her cell. She laughed her appreciation. We knew we were in a situation beyond our control but we did not feel abandoned by God. Every so often a student prayed. Someone else cracked open a chess set and we became absorbed in talking strategy around the board. It became an oddly relaxed evening. The calm between the storm of the restaurant raid and the news we received the next day that the secret police were, indeed, pressing charges and that several of the team were facing potential jail sentences.

THE LEAGUE OF ASSORTED ODDBALLS

That night, as I lay on my bed in the train's sleeping compartment, listening to the rhythmic clicking of wheels against track as we fled for safety, my mind wandered to another time and place. Far less dramatic but, in its own way, also intensely challenging. I could picture myself sat on a hard plastic chair in a small classroom with eleven other students. We were in a circle listening to someone give a short talk; a few moments earlier we'd been playing some silly games as a way to get to know one another.

Three of us were in our second week of university, the rest were in the years above us. We constituted the only Christian society on our campus of several thousand students. As far as we knew, there were no more than one or two other students openly following Jesus in the whole institution. Coming from a small church, and having only experienced the transforming power of God for myself a few months earlier, I had hoped that maybe my student years would be the time when I got to know lots of other believers. Perhaps I would find people who shared my interests as well as my experience of God. But here we were – a dozen random strangers with little in common aside from our faith, gathered beneath the cold fluorescent lights of a seminar room. It didn't quite seem like I was living the dream.

Ten days previously I had been sat on the edge of my bed, staring at six cardboard boxes and one large bag. These contained my clothing, books, stationery, stereo and computer. The material objects transported in the back of my parents' hatchback as I began life in a new city. I'd spent my preceding fifteen years living in the same house, in a small village which seemed to have more cows than people, and with my grandmother just down the road; my father had been the PE teacher at my school. I knew it would be impossible to reproduce that sense of home in a new setting instantly, yet even I was shocked by the level of disorientation I felt as my parents drove away. All I could do was cry.

The only common area in our hall of residence was the kitchen, and nobody seemed to be cooking that week. Those I met in passing seemed to be busy emptying their bank accounts in bars and takeaways around the city. It was hard to begin figuring out how to connect with people whose lives seemed so centred on consuming alcohol and enjoying casual sex. Over my years as a student I would come to discover that this intensely hedonistic period at the beginning of British university life dies down over the course of first year: the need to actually study, along with financial pressures and mounting regret over hasty relationship decisions, tends to calm and focus the lives of most undergraduates.

But I wasn't to know any of this. It simply felt isolating. I had no intention of indulging in alcohol-soaked sensual shenanigans, and so I felt like a fringe character in the life of the university. I was naturally a little bit shy and uncertain in social situations but I'd never been without people I trusted before. Suddenly, though, the simple task of making friends had become a paralyzing challenge. I joined the university hockey club, a sport I'd played throughout secondary school, and discovered that initiation into the group required consuming vast amounts of beer as part of a humiliating ceremony. So I went to practices but struggled to crack the social aspect of team life.

Even academic life was challenging. My degree was in elementary education, something from which I would later switch in favour of English Literature, and I immediately discovered that the lecturer for the religious education module was intensely anti-Christian. He took every possible opportunity, even in our first two classes, to depict belief in the Bible as naïve and untenable in the modern world. It seemed like even the classroom wasn't destined to be a comfortable place. It was for this reason that I found the Christian Union talk in the seminar room hard to take seriously. The speaker, who seemed like a lovely and sincere person, was trying to paint a verbal picture of what it meant to live as a follower of Jesus at university. Her upbeat tone was utterly at odds with my own feelings of struggle and discomfort.

When she told us that our student years could be 'a time of amazing spiritual growth', it took some effort for me not to snort aloud with laughter. I found the very idea comical – that I, facing relational isolation, academic discomfort and a heavy sense of loss for all I had left behind in my comfortable village home, could somehow flourish in this setting. It seemed inconceivable. Looking around at the eleven other people in the room hardly helped me take heart. If this, our tiny league of assorted oddballs, was the Christian community on campus then surely – I surmised – my prospects of 'spiritual growth' were slim.

HOW IT ALWAYS HAPPENS

It turned out that I couldn't be more wrong. In the two decades which followed I came to see this meeting, and those awkward first weeks on campus, as my entry point into a dynamic global work of God. I was joining a movement spanning 160 different nations and encompassing over half a million students. It would lead me around the world and to committing many years of my life to founding and developing new Christian communities on previously-unreached university campuses. Eventually, it had brought me to a fold-down bed in a shaky carriage speeding through the icy night and away from the secret police, where I could lie back and remember that small gathering on campus with warm gratitude. Despite the danger of that evening, I was still thankful to have been drawn into something of more value than even my personal safety and well-being.

When the train arrived at its destination, I took a taxi to a monastery on the outskirts of town. I hid out there for a day before reconvening with the organizers in a city-centre pizza restaurant. It had been a restless night for me as every footstep or sound in the corridor outside had raised my pulse and pricked my imagination with dark possibilities. My friends had endured the same experience. Fear of a knock at the door, they told me, was one of the tools of the secret police's trade and they were known to delay actual arrests so as to accentuate the tension felt by their targets. Yet, as in our prayer meeting the morning after the raid, what concerned them most was that their freedom to proclaim Jesus was being threatened by unexpectedly becoming the subject of government attention. Jail could be survived; having to keep Jesus to themselves seemed intolerable.

As I looked across the table at them, images flashed through my mind of a day outside Jerusalem which I've read about many times. Eleven friends of Jesus stood blinking as he disappeared from their midst.[2] They were now – according to his final words – the ones who would live and speak for him in his physical absence. None of them had formal theological training and there was not an ordained priest or rabbi among them. Several were expert fishermen, if that helped; muscled chaps who could weather a storm and haul in a waterlogged net, but hardly the kind of folk you would choose to give speeches and pen documents for launching a global movement. Sure, some of them would become well-known figures over time: Peter, Thomas, James and John, for example, are still lodged in the consciousness of most Christians, even two millennia later. Andrew, who tradition holds ranged around Eastern Europe proclaiming Jesus, eventually became the patron saint of lands as distant from his birthplace as Barbados, Scotland and the Philippines. But they didn't start out this way.

The eleven were likely young when Jesus ascended. Possibly many of them were no more than twenty years

---

2 Acts 1:4–9.

old.[3] The Christian faith would remain as either illegal or a fringe renewal movement of Judaism for all their lives. Their preaching frequently occurred under a looming threat of violence: James was the first among the eleven to lose his life, his head hacked off with a sword on royal orders.[4] Most of the others would eventually perish in similarly gruesome fashion at the hands of mobs or ruthless local governments.[5] Their experiences, in fact, were shared by many of Jesus' other followers beyond the eleven – death stalked the early Christians around the Roman Empire as they spread the way of Jesus. Well before John was penning the final letters of the New Testament from enforced exile on a small Greek island, the Roman Emperor Nero had taken to nailing Christians to crosses and setting them on fire as a way to illuminate his night-time garden parties.[6] Things didn't get much better under his successors.

---

3 The age of the disciples is not directly cited in the New Testament accounts, but they are generally assumed to be relatively young. Considering that the twelve are following as teacher a man generally agreed to be in his early thirties, it's reasonable to assume that they were somewhat younger. Rabbinical conventions, which Jesus – of course – may well have broken, dictated that one would become disciple to a teacher while still in one's teens. John, assuming it is he who wrote Revelation, also lived until close to the end of the first century, suggesting he was also young when physically with Jesus. Some also point to the fact that in Matthew 17:24–27 only Peter and Jesus pay the temple tax, which according to Exodus 30:14 was due only from 'those twenty years old or more'. This interpretation, though, relies on the assumption that the other disciples had not already paid, a matter on which the text is silent. I've come across no advocates for them being older than their twenties.

4 Acts 12:1–2.

5 For a detailed academic exploration of this issue, see: Sean McDowell, The Fate of the Apostles: Examining the Martyrdom Accounts of the Closest Followers of Jesus (Routledge, 2015).

6 Anthony A. Barrett, Elaine Fantham & John C. Yardley (eds.), The Emperor Nero: A Guide to the Ancient Sources (Princeton University Press, 2016), pp.167–168.

As I sat with my friends, waiting on our pizza order, I was conscious of being among some of the eleven's contemporary successors – young followers of Jesus whose government tosses constant obstacles in the way of them proclaiming him. Yet, like James, John and the rest of the eleven, they consider obedience to Jesus more valuable than their own comfort. And, like me – surrounded by oddballs beneath the fluorescent lights of a mostly-empty seminar room – they had stumbled upon a handful of collaborators who would be with them as they lived and spoke for Jesus in their university, and among the student body.

STUDENT MOVEMENT

Such collaborative Christian student communities exist on campuses around the world. Some, like the Nigeria Fellowship of Evangelical Students (NIFES), span hundreds of campuses and see thousands attend their national conferences. Others are buried so far underground they don't officially exist. Though they stand in a tradition stretching back to the eleven, the global student movements profiled in this book began to take shape in the late 1940s on the campus of Harvard University.[7] Delegates of nationally-led Christian student networks from ten countries came

---

[7] For the details of this historical section, I am leaning heavily on two books, and this whole section is a selective précis of the relevant sections from: Pete Lowman, *The Day of His Power: A History of the International Fellowship of Evangelical Students* (IVP, 1983), and A. Donald MacLeod, *C. Stacey Woods and the Evangelical Rediscovery of the University* (IVP Academic, 2007). More recent figures and information come from internal IFES statistics supplied to me by IFES Associate General Secretary Tim Adams in December 2018. Timothée Joset of Groupes Bibliques des Ecoles et Universités in Switzerland, whose PhD thesis at Durham University covers the history and theology of IFES, also fact-checked this section.

together for seven days in August 1947. Australia, Britain, Canada, China, France, Holland, New Zealand, Norway, Switzerland and the United States were all represented. They decided together to begin the International Fellowship of Evangelical Students (IFES).

Evangelical student movements had been forming around the world over the preceding thirty years. Many had emerged after the two major international student movements of the late nineteenth century – the Student Volunteer Movement (SVM) and the Student Christian Movement (SCM) – had sidelined the core tenets of the Christian faith in favour of unity based mainly around activism. In 1910, SCM General Secretary Tissington Tatlow had gone so far as to say that his movement had no interest in defining 'what is orthodox and what is not orthodox'.[8] Many SVM folk retained their own evangelical convictions throughout this period, but the movement's overall accent shifted in another direction. Adrift from basic convictions about Christ's saving power or the authority of the Scriptures, they rapidly lost interest in inviting others to follow Jesus and the imperative to reach out stagnated.

The former SCM affiliates at Cambridge University and in the medical schools of London withdrew from the organization and soon others joined them.[9] A new network, formed in 1928 as Inter-Varsity Fellowship (IVF) and today known as the Universities and Colleges Christian Fellowship (UCCF), began. Similar events occurred in Norway, as students formed the Norges Kristelige Studentlag (NKS, now NKSS), into which they folded much of the former

---

8 Lowman, *The Day of His Power*, p.38.

9 CICCU actually predates SCM by twelve years.

Norwegian SVM. In Switzerland, Bible studies and camps for students emerged in a variety of locations, with a more recognizable structure emerging by 1932.

New student movements in the English-speaking world soon cascaded out from the United Kingdom as IVF commissioned Howard Guinness, a medical graduate of St Bartholomew's Hospital in London, to travel to Canada and meet with contacts made there by one of their founders. Guinness was armed with just a one-way boat ticket, £14 and a heavy overcoat to help him survive the Canadian winter. Traversing Canada by train, he brought together Christian students in a succession of universities across the nation, and within a year helped form Inter-Varsity Christian Fellowship of Canada (IVCF Canada). Guinness was then telegraphed by a Sydney-based businessman and, at his invitation, travelled to Australia and New Zealand to help students there launch local groups and national networks. While in Australia, he recruited twenty-four-year-old Stacey Woods to go and lead IVCF Canada. Within a few years, Woods would also help launch Inter-Varsity Christian Fellowship in the United States (IVCF USA).

Regular 'International Conferences' bringing together students, academics and supportive church leaders from various emerging student movements began at the behest of the Norwegians in 1934. Throughout the decade, students travelled to visit each other's movements and Christian academics embarked on speaking tours in one another's nations. The last of the 'International Conferences', with thirty-three nations represented, occurred in 1939. A few months later, the Second World War disrupted international communication for a period and everyone became focused on their own context. Havoc was wrought on some movements during the war. Theologian Ole Hallesby, a founder of the Norwegian movement and later the first President of IFES, spent much of the war in jail for protesting the deportation of Jewish and other Norwegian youth to Nazi Germany. Other movements were completely crushed, not to re-emerge for decades.

But the period was not entirely destructive to Christian work among the universities: a French and Dutch student movement emerged during and after the Nazi occupation, as did another in China towards the end of the war. The Swiss movement – then encompassing both German and French-speaking regions – also formally constituted itself in 1942.[10] Each were led by locals. When the conflict ended, these four new movements, along with the four pioneered in the 1930s by Guinness and Woods, joined together with the British IVF and Norwegian NKS to arrange the August 1947 Harvard gathering. It was decided that, instead of simply holding another 'International Conference' in the pre-war vein, they would instead take the opportunity to recognize and constitute themselves into a coherent and identifiable international movement. And so the International Fellowship of Evangelical Students was born.

The choice of the word 'Fellowship' was intentional – it was to be a network of equals, with each movement led by nationals, and yet with a generous sharing of resources, both human and financial. Renowned Welsh preacher Martyn Lloyd-Jones, the first Chairman of IFES and the main speaker at the 1947 Harvard conference, had spent the previous two years chairing a group which had drafted a basic statement of faith – a 'doctrinal basis' – which struck

---

10 Switzerland now has two distinct movements, one each for German and French-speaking regions.

a fine balance between clarifying evangelical essentials and also leaving room for IFES members and staff to differ on secondary issues and belong to a range of churches.[11] It was agreed that IFES would not become a hierarchical organization but would focus on facilitating and supporting one another's work across national borders. Any structures which developed would be supportive rather than directive.

IFES has remained, over the decades that followed, close to its founding principles. Most movements are still nationally-led. Those which are not are usually recently-founded ones, whose initiators are working on transitioning to local leadership in the near future. The first four General Secretaries of IFES have each been drawn from a different continent: Stacey Woods (Australian, 1947–1971), Chua Wee Hian (Singaporean, 1971–1991), Lindsay Brown (Welsh, 1991–2007), and Daniel Bourdanné (Chadian, 2007–present). IFES has also retained its evangelical character, as expressed in the doctrinal basis, and continues to include people from a wide range of church backgrounds. The early emphasis on student initiative, evident in the fact that people like Howard Guinness and Stacey Woods were advising and networking local campus-based groups as much as they were initiating them, is also still a feature of IFES. Students ordinarily lead on campus, while staff advise and support.

In other ways the movement has changed greatly. From just ten constituent member movements, IFES has grown

---

11 Christopher Catherwood, *Martyn Lloyd-Jones: His Life and Relevance for the 21st Century* (IVP, 2015), pp.95–100. The statement of faith was very similar to one drafted by Lloyd-Jones for London Bible College: see Ian M. Randall, *Educating Evangelicalism: The Origins, Development and Impact of London Bible College* (Paternoster Press, 2000), p.27.

to over 160. Some – such as in Finland and Sweden – were already in contact with the IFES founders and affiliated not long after the Harvard meeting. Others – such as in Japan or Israel – grew up locally and then came to hear of IFES and requested membership. Still others – such as in Sri Lanka – emerged when nationals returned home from studies in cities with established IFES movements and decided to start their own. And, of course, pioneering from outsiders remains important: Indians planted the student movement in Nepal, Indonesians initiated the Cambodian work and Trinidadians founded the first group in Grenada. The 1990s were possibly the most explosive period of growth in IFES history as relative freedom of religion spread across Eastern and Central Europe, as well as much of Eurasia, and student numbers expanded fourfold in some African nations, leading to forty-nine new movements joining during these ten years.

After I first encountered IFES in its local form as a UCCF-supported Christian Union, my initial scepticism – so strongly felt as I listened to the speaker paint a picture of student life as a time of potential spiritual flourishing – soon gave way to deep appreciation. This small community helped shape the way I viewed and interacted with the university environment. It moved me from intimidation to engagement. Before long, I was speaking up when my lecturer attacked the Christian faith – gently raising questions which showed my colleagues that perhaps the whole thing was not as irrational as they were being told. This opened up conversations after class and I began finding ways to build on those connections without compromising the lifestyle to which I was committed. Some of these new friends even came to a series of events our little group ran on campus offering newcomers a chance to investigate Jesus for themselves. Within three months, I had prayed with one of my fellow students as he became a follower of Jesus.

When I switched subjects after my first semester I moved to a larger institution, Cardiff University, where the Christian Union numbered almost 200 students. This opened the opportunity for me to hear about the global IFES network for the first time when Lindsay Brown – then the IFES General Secretary – came and spoke at our weekly meeting. He told of how new student groups were popping up all over Eastern Europe in the aftermath of communism's collapse and how they needed support. My imagination was captured by what I heard and I approached the local UCCF staff worker asking if she could help me get out there to be part of what was happening. She connected me with a summer team drawn from Christian Unions across Wales and Ireland, and we spent several weeks together that July helping the recently-founded Slovakian student movement run camps where students could learn English and also find out more about Jesus.

A year later, I ran into the leader of that summer team, Beth, at a conference, and she asked me what I was doing after graduation. When I explained my plans, which involved being trained and mentored by a national evangelist, she nodded politely, then told me, 'You need to go and work with students in mainland Europe – I think you have a gift there.' I laughed aloud even at the idea. My future was set and it looked good. It turned out, over the following months, that God agreed with Beth and he was calling me back to Eastern Europe for the longer-term.

This all led to three years working alongside the Romanian student movement, OSCER, which had been founded just three years previously. Then it was back to the

UK for five years with UCCF, which overlapped with three years of being contracted to write articles about evangelism for the website of IVCF USA. During those stints of working with IFES, I've had the privilege of helping several new groups launch which are still continuing today.

These days I don't work *for* IFES, but much of what I do is *in collaboration* with them: our little organization, Chrysolis, is focused on partnering with existing locally-led Christian organizations and churches to stimulate conversation about Jesus in public settings such as universities. One aspect of our work includes connection with the Fellowship of Evangelists in the Universities of Europe (FEUER), the IFES-linked network of those involved in public communication about Jesus around the continent. It was at FEUER's annual gathering that I first met my Eurasian friends, who invited me to speak at their restaurant-based event. When we met they told me how their national student movement had begun just ten years earlier, and had swiftly spread to several cities. Every year they hold more than ten university outreach weeks, despite their work being under constant pressure from those in authority. They continue the pioneering spirit of early IFES, as the city in which I spoke doesn't even have an organized Christian student group yet – just four or five undergraduate friends who want to see something happen. The restaurant outreach was designed to help facilitate the new group's launch.

CAMPUS LIGHTS

While the event's organizers and I ate pizza together, mine topped with some particularly tangy banana peppers, we talked about how a meeting had been arranged for the next day with a lawyer. He would assess their chances of evading prison and help them prepare for their eventual arrest. As our conversation continued and drifted away from imminent legal peril, the eyes of my friend – who had also been my translator in the restaurant – alighted on a notebook and fountain pen, placed just to my left on the table. She asked me about it and I explained that it was my journal. I had been scribbling down some of my thoughts about the past few days, while they were still fresh in my mind. She laughed warmly.

I knew exactly why she was amused. A few days earlier, as we traipsed through the snow, unaware that we were hours away from having our event closed down by the police, I had been sharing with her about a book I would be writing. It was, I explained, to be the literary equivalent of a TED Talk on global student movements. I planned to travel to a range of countries and to conduct over a hundred interviews so that I could gather stories. It was just two weeks since I had agreed with IFES and my publisher, Muddy Pearl, to begin work on the research and I was curious as to what I would uncover over the coming months. As my friend looked at my journal and laughed, she said to me, 'Well, I guess you have your first story.'

She was right and I am thankful that she encouraged its inclusion in the final draft. Many more stories were to follow soon after, and the easiest way for you to find those is to keep turning the pages and continue reading. What you hold in your hands is a journalistic account of what God is doing in tertiary institutions and among students around the world. Its aim is to inspire and inform you. One of the things I have always loved about IFES is when students and staff come together at conferences and other communal events and swap stories with one another. As you read this book, it will be the equivalent of listening in on such conversations with numerous people from fourteen different IFES-linked Christian student movements, spanning every region of the globe.[12] I am a cultural outsider to most countries in this book, though I have personally visited the majority, and I am sure there are many nuances I overlook as a result of my own cultural vantage point. All the stories featured, though, have been approved and fact-checked by the people involved and I have made corrections and changes wherever suggested.[13]

Campus Lights is aimed at anybody wanting to hear stories of God at work. I'm guessing that is likely primarily to be those already following Jesus. If you wouldn't consider yourself a Christian – and I'm guessing, at the very least, some of my friends and family may read this just out of curiosity, as they do some of my other writing – then know that I assume a sympathy towards the way of Jesus on the part of my readers. Hopefully the language is free of excessive Christian jargon, or 'Christianese', but I don't attempt to justify or argue for the way followers of Jesus

---

12 IFES is organized into eleven administrative regions and I have been careful to select a country from each region. The regions are: Caribbean, English-and-Portuguese-Speaking Africa, East Asia, Eurasia, Europe, Francophone Africa, Latin America, Middle East and North Africa, North America, South Asia, South Pacific. For more information, visit the IFES website at ifesworld.org.

13 For clarity's sake regarding the fourteen countries included in this book: I grew up in Britain, currently live in Romania, studied part-time for my MA in the USA and have been formally attached to the IFES movements in each of these three countries in some form. I also personally visited Indonesia, Guatemala, Mongolia and Burkina Faso, as well as the unnamed Middle Eastern and Eurasian countries featured in this book. The research on South Korea, Sri Lanka, the Solomon Islands, and St Kitts occurred without me visiting personally and – inevitably – ended up undergoing the most revision during earlier drafts, thanks to the kind input and suggestions from folks in those and associated movements.

see the world. There are lots of other good books out there which do that![14] Though, that said, I hope that you at least find the contents of this book intriguing. It's an odd feature of my life that when I give public talks and presentations, they are ordinarily in non-church settings like universities, schools, bars and theatres, and I am usually addressing and interacting with overwhelmingly non-Christian audiences – often quite sceptical ones – but both this and my previous book are addressed towards those already following Jesus.[15] Maybe my next writing project will be geared towards a different kind of audience. In the meantime, feel free to email me if you want to engage on anything which comes up in this book.[16]

One set of readers who, I think, will especially enjoy this book are those presently or previously involved in a Christian student group. When I joined the Christian Union during my first intimidating undergraduate weeks, I had no idea that I was part of something huge and global. I've noticed many Christian students have the same experience – they are very involved with the group on their own campus, but are only vaguely aware of what happens beyond. *Campus Lights* is designed to provide you with some inspiration as you seek to engage with your own setting. Through the narratives in this book I hope you will be challenged to consider afresh how you – both the singular and plural 'you'; the latter meaning 'you together with the other followers of Jesus on your campus' – live

---

14 See, for example: Tim Keller, *Making Sense of God: An Invitation to the Skeptical* (Hodder, 2018).

15 Luke Cawley, *The Myth of the Non-Christian: Engaging Atheists, Nominal Christians and the Spiritual But Not Religious* (IVP, 2016).

16 luke@chrysolis.org.

and speak for him where you are studying. At the end of each chapter I have added some reflection questions to help readers, student or otherwise, to consider the implications of what they have read.

This is not a book of 'best practice'. Nor is it a string of flawless success stories. I've instead done my best to convey the sense of struggle and setback which can often occur in work among students. So I'm not suggesting that readers copy everything they find in the pages that follow. Hopefully, though, you can read it and ask yourself, 'How could we do that *kind of thing*, only in a way which fits in our context?' Consider *Campus Lights* a tool for developing your 'missional imagination' with regard to the possibilities for your setting. To that end, you will find I've also blended into each chapter some brief reflections from the New Testament. They are intended as a complement to the book's more contemporary stories, and each one takes a single incident from an eight-week window in the first century – between Jesus' entry into Jerusalem on a donkey and the descent of the Spirit at Pentecost – and uses it as the starting point for an imaginative narrative exploration of how the Scriptures speak to the themes of the chapter. Contemplation on Jesus' life and teaching is, in my experience, the most helpful way to develop one's own understanding of what it means to participate in his mission.

You'll notice that I have restricted my contemporary stories to those from tertiary institutions – tales of undergraduates, graduates and academics.[17] Many IFES

---

17 Friends from New Zealand and Ireland, among other places, tend to describe tertiary institutions by various specific labels; 'universities', 'polytechnics', 'colleges', etc. I, like most Brits of my generation, have a habit of grouping all such places under the single heading of 'universities', and you'll notice I stick to this usage throughout most of the book.

movements also work in secondary schools and even sometimes in primary schools. But those are topics for another book. In *Campus Lights*, each chapter focuses on a single aspect of *tertiary* student ministry, and echoes one of IFES' six 'strategic priorities'.[18] The first four are all about impact:

1. Inviting others to follow Jesus.
2. Engaging contemporary issues.
3. Involving ourselves in the university setting.
4. Integration between students and graduates.

The final two are about necessary elements of making this impact sustainable:

5. Leadership development.
6. Financial viability.

Together they form quite a nice summary of a student movement's basic tasks. As one former IFES General Secretary commented to me: 'They're what we should all be doing anyway.'

One of the things I love, when I spend time with IFES students, is how frequently I encounter a raw passion for speaking of Jesus. This is especially true in the lives of my Eurasian friends. The day after our meeting over pizza we found ourselves crammed into a small and messy city-centre flat, legal books literally spilling off many of the

---

18 The strategic priorities can be found in *Living Stones*, a document produced by IFES in 2008, which aims to outline what is needed for student-led missional communities to keep growing in the world's universities. See the summary of *Living Stones* in Appendix Two.

brown, wooden shelves. It was here that we discovered from my friend's lawyer that the maximum sentence for organizing an illegal religious event was ninety days in jail. Over the months that followed, I kept in touch with my Eurasian friends via various social media platforms from back home in Bucharest, Romania, where I currently live with my family. They kept telling me that their main concern was not jail time but the possibility that the legal process would render it even harder to speak publicly of Jesus in the future.

Each person was eventually charged in their hometown. Three of the event's organizers went through a full trial back in the capital city. A recording of my unfinished talk was played to the courtroom as my friends looked on from the iron cage in which defendants have to sit. The judge became increasingly sympathetic with each passing day of proceedings. She wasn't in a position, however, to find them 'not guilty': when the secret police bring the charges there is only one possible verdict. Instead she convicted them, but then issued the lowest possible penalty – a fine so small it wouldn't even cover three cups of coffee.

A few months later my friends were back at it again. Their next week of outreach events happened directly across the street from the capital city courtroom and streams of students came to hear about Jesus. Some even joined Bible studies and subsequently became followers of Jesus. Meanwhile, back in the city where I couldn't even get halfway through a talk without the police silencing me, a fresh attempt to develop a student group is already being discussed. They, in the darkness, will be the lights of their campus.

QUESTIONS FOR REFLECTION OR DISCUSSION:

What is your present or past involvement, if any, in Christian student movements at the local, regional, national or international level? What one story from your personal experience most encapsulates what you have encountered so far?

What in this chapter most resonated with your own experience, or gave you pause to think?

Do you normally conceive of your life, and that of your Christian community, as the contemporary continuation of the stories in the New Testament? Jot down some ways you see continuity and discontinuity between what you know of events then and your experience now.

CHAPTER TWO:
DREAMS AND
CHRISTMAS TREES

TALES OF PROCLAIMING JESUS
(INDONESIA AND THE MIDDLE EAST)

She was literally sweating with fear. In the darkness of her bedroom, Pepper[19] fought to bring her rapid breathing under control. The dream had been so very graphic. It had begun with her mother cleaning the house – not typically promising material for a nightmare – yet, as she worked her way around the building, ever closer to Pepper's room, the tension rose. Time seemed to slow down as Pepper helplessly watched her mother open her blue wooden wardrobe, reach inside, and pull out a wooden cross, an object so shameful its discovery jolted her back into the waking world, bringing only her terror with her.

Pepper couldn't shake the memory of the dream even as she headed off to class that day. It kept replaying in her head as she tried to concentrate on economics lectures and group discussions. By the time she reached the coffee shop that evening she was itching to share it with her friends. It

---

[19] All names of people from Indonesia and the Middle East have been changed in this chapter.

was normal for them to spend the hour after class talking together and it had become the natural place for them all to share whatever was on their minds. No topic was off limits – love, hopes, fears, books, movies, any random humorous thoughts which just popped into their minds. Tonight, for the second time in the past few months, their focus was going to be dream interpretation. She wondered if what she had seen was a message from God.

As Pepper told me later, it's not so rare to discuss God in Indonesia; almost everybody has a religion and the nation was founded as a monotheistic state which granted liberty for all to practice and express their own convictions.[20] There are sometimes tensions between Christians and Muslims – even violent clashes in some regions – but in Jakarta, where Pepper studied, mosques and churches are often intentionally built across the street from one another as a gesture of friendship between the two faith communities. Around eighty-seven per cent of the population is officially Muslim, but both Protestants (seven per cent) and Catholics (three per cent) have legal protections enshrined in law.[21]

Pepper was the sole Muslim among her small group of coffee-loving Christian friends. She'd never felt any pressure from them to adopt their viewpoint. Quite the opposite; it was *she*, at the beginning of their friendship, who had tried to convince *them* of Islam. She told me that she actually felt sorry for them. They seemed like such lovely people.

---

20 Two books which especially helped me understand the Indonesian religious and political context are: M.C. Ricklefs, *A History of Modern Indonesia since c. 1200 (Fourth Edition)* (Palgrave Macmillan, 2008) and Jan Sihar Aritonang & Karel Steenbrink (eds.), *A History of Christianity in Indonesia* (Brill, 2008).

21 Based on the results of the 2010 Indonesia census: 'Population by Region and Religion', *Badan Pusat Statistik: Sensus Penduduk 2010*, https://sp2010.bps. go.id (Accessed 28 March 2019).

How could they be so lost and so wrong about something as important as God? She wanted to help them discover the truth. Over time, though, she began to find that their counterarguments were stronger than she expected. Plus, they seemed genuinely to love her, regardless of what she thought about God. A question slowly began to gnaw away at the back of her mind; 'If I was not born a Muslim, what would I believe?'

Then came her first conversation with them about dreams: one night she had seen a hill with three crosses on it and her unfamiliarity with the gospel narratives meant that she didn't know what these represented. But it felt significant. When she shared it with her Christian friends they explained to her about the death of Jesus and how, for them, it signified God paying the cost of reconciling humanity back to himself. So intrigued was she by this idea that it catapulted her into reading a series of books about Jesus recommended by her friends. Nabeel Qureshi's *Seeking Allah, Finding Jesus* – the first-hand story of a young Muslim investigating Jesus for himself – was one which resonated particularly deeply with her.[22] She also read the stories of Jesus in the New Testament for the first time and talked these through with her friends as she did.

By the time she had her second dream – the traumatic one where her mother pulled a giant wooden cross from her blue bedroom wardrobe – she was torn in two directions. It seemed to her like the dream symbolized the way she kept her growing attraction to Jesus hidden away from her devoutly Muslim parents. The Christian books she was reading lay hidden around her room, covered in

---

22 Nabeel Qureshi, *Seeking Allah, Finding Jesus: A Devout Muslim Encounters Christianity* (Zondervan, 2018).

patterned wrapping paper so that family members wouldn't spy them and ask awkward questions. As she explained the dream and the thoughts it had triggered to her friends, they began talking together about Jesus. Pepper particularly remembers one of her friends, Alex, making an offhand reference to an incident involving the Pharisees. Alex recounted Jesus' critique of them as diligent rule-keepers who were somehow disconnected from God. It was, she told me, like he was describing her.

Pepper couldn't think about much else over the days that followed. Everything finally came to a head some days later in her locked bedroom as she was reading a small book of daily reflections on biblical texts. The words 'Be still, and know that I am God'[23] jumped out at her with unexpected force. Pepper realized that, instead of resisting Jesus any longer, she needed to admit that she'd become convinced by what she had read in the New Testament, experienced through her dreams and seen in her friends' lives. It was time to trust him. She found herself speaking directly to Jesus for the first time and welcoming him into her life, asking his forgiveness, and committing herself to follow him.

Talking to Jesus as if he were presently alive and in possession of divine attributes (such as the power to forgive) clearly moved her far outside orthodox Islam; it seemed more like Christianity. The next day, at their normal coffee spot, Pepper broke the news to her Christian friends. They listened with joy as Pepper, still wearing her hijab, explained that she was now a firmly committed follower of Jesus. Amidst their excitement, her friends also cautioned

---

23 Psalm 46:10.

her to wait before she went public with this news. Not even her family should know. They suggested she should keep wearing her hijab and attending the mosque for a while yet. The consequences of not doing so, they warned, could be disastrous.

FREEDOM TO CHOOSE

At first glance this seems like strange advice. Why, in a modern pluralistic city like Jakarta, would it be such a problem for a student to change their mind on what they believe about God? Christians are hardly a beleaguered underground group. We're not talking about ISIS-occupied Iraq. I have attended Christian student meetings at the heart of a Muslim-majority university campus in Jakarta and witnessed their enthusiastic singing and forthright biblical preaching. The doors and windows of the meeting room were all open and any student passing by could have heard the songs and words about Jesus; yet there was not even a hint of fear among those Christians present.

Freedom to practise Christian worship personally, though, is not quite the same as liberty to invite others to do the same. Some Indonesian Christian students told me a story about how they were running an outreach event on their campus and had publicized it through a series of posters. A female student in a hijab was intrigued by the event's title and decided to come along. Two days later, the leaders of the Christian group were hauled up before the university authorities and 'given a very strict warning' that if any Muslim was seen attending their meetings again then they would lose their right to meet on campus. The likely tensions arising from a Muslim even seeming to edge towards Christianity were not, they were told, something the university was willing to risk.

Staff of Perkantas, the Indonesian Christian student movement, told me that these restrictions place them in a seemingly unwinnable situation. Either they confine their meetings only to Christians – and perhaps those from the country's other religious minorities, such as Hindus or Buddhists, whose dress does not obviously mark them out as non-Christian – or they face the loss of freedom to operate on university property. I was initially tempted, when I first met the Perkantas staff, simply to urge them towards greater boldness and disregard for the consequences. But this would almost inevitably mean the Christian community entirely losing any public presence within the university. With each conversation I began to see more clearly the depth of their dilemma. Was it, they constantly asked themselves, worth gambling their few current freedoms on campus for the likely outcome of losing them all? The answer is far from straightforward.

This quandary is hardly unique to Indonesia. Conversion is an incendiary issue in every Muslim-majority nation. Most such cultures are comfortable with others *being* Christians, but tend to be deeply hostile to one of their own *becoming* a Christian. Indonesia is probably as liberal as it gets on this issue. In many of these countries, moving from Islam to Christianity is legally punishable by death or prison, and can often result in losing custody of one's own children.[24] Some of this is rooted in the traditional Islamic teaching that 'apostasy' – abandoning Islam – is the most heinous

---

[24] This is fairly common knowledge, but for some details on various countries, see: 'Laws Criminalizing Apostasy', *The Library of Congress*, https://www.loc. gov/law/help/apostasy/ (Accessed 28 March 2019).

of all sins. But the situation is also, ironically, compounded by laws originally designed to protect Christian minorities.

Many other Islamic-majority countries, following an ancient precedent set by Zoroastrian[25] Persia in its kindly treatment of early Christians, have multiple legal systems which coexist within the same nation. Each country will have a common criminal code which applies to all citizens but will then permit each religious group to collectively set its own laws on issues like marriage, divorce, burial, inheritance and child custody. Every citizen is obliged to be part of one group, be it Jewish, Roman Catholic, Protestant, Muslim or any other category available in a given country.[26]

The system was designed to carve a space for freedom of conscience among religious minorities, but over the years it has become near-impossible to disentangle oneself legally from the religious identity with which one is born. Many Muslims who become followers of Jesus don't even bother with the legalities and instead retain an official identity as Muslims, despite following Jesus and even joining churches.

Evangelism, which is the practice of communicating about Jesus with invitational intent, tends to be central to most IFES student groups. They see themselves as existing largely to make Jesus known among their colleagues. Lindsay Brown, the former General Secretary of IFES, often

---

25 Zoroastrianism is the ancient, pre-Islamic religion of Iran that still exists in India (the followers now known as Parsees) and in isolated areas of Iran.

26 For more details, see: Jonathan Andrews, *Identity Crisis: Religious Registration in the Middle East* (Gilead Books, 2016); or the summary of this in: Jonathan Andrews, 'Living as a Christian, Registered as a Muslim?: Violence and Discrimination against Middle East Christians', *Lausanne Global Analysis, March 2017, Volume 6, Issue 2*, https://www.lausanne.org/content/lga/2017-03/living-as-a-christian-registered-as-a-muslim, (Accessed 28 March 2019). This isn't the case in Indonesia.

says that effective student movements invite others to follow Jesus in three ways: through interpersonal friendships, via small groups which look at the gospels together and through public proclamation. Pepper experienced the first and the second as she spoke and looked at the stories of Jesus with her coffee-drinking student friends. It is Lindsay's third category – public proclamation – which poses the greatest challenge for a context like Indonesia.[27] How can we possibly undertake public evangelism in a setting where conversion is either functionally or formally illegal, and where those groups which do meet on campus are liable to be ejected the moment they attempt outreach? It seems impossible.

EVERYWHERE IS OPEN

Surprisingly, I have learned that even the most hostile of settings can be engaged publicly. I was recently discussing situations like Indonesia with Sri Lankan theologian Vinoth Ramachandra, a key early leader of the student movement in his country, when he made a remark which stayed with me; he said that, 'There is no such thing as a closed or unreachable campus.' When I asked him what he meant by that, he explained that so long as Christian students are permitted to study at a university, they have the opportunity to speak publicly of Jesus. This might be in the context of classroom discussions or it could be through involvement

---

27 It's worth emphasizing that my research and contacts in Indonesia were in Jakarta, and the stories I tell here are local to that setting. I did my best to understand the national situation, but both Indonesia and Perkantas are vast and so it is difficult to generalize about either one. Were this chapter to focus instead on the Indonesian province of Bali, which is eighty-three per cent Hindu, then the set of challenges and opportunities would be different. But I chose to focus this chapter on majority-Muslim contexts.

in the life of the university. But we must be cautious not to assume that inability to run and host specifically Christian meetings on campus means that proclamation of Jesus is automatically rendered impossible.

Mariam is a great example of this – she studies literature in the capital city of a ninety-five per cent Muslim-majority Middle Eastern nation, and told me that she is regularly permitted to speak about her faith during lectures and seminars by Islamic professors. Students in her city face far greater restrictions than are experienced anywhere in Indonesia, and could certainly never meet publicly on campus. Yet the door opens for Mariam because so many classic European texts touch upon the topic of Christianity. Who can fully grasp Brontë, Donne, Dickens or Eliot – let alone Tolstoy, Hugo or Dostoevsky – without some grasp of the Christian faith? Mariam regularly interjects, sometimes even at the request of her professors, to clarify or explain a particular point of doctrine or Scripture as they arise in the assigned class texts. As the only follower of Jesus in most of her classes, she is automatically viewed as a voice of authority on Christian practice and experience.

Mariam says she was even able to share her own experience of God when the topic of Christian prayer was touched upon in one Victorian novel. She told the class about her prayer journal, in which she records 'small miracles' which occur in her life as she prays in Jesus' name. The teacher asked her to explain more about some of these events, which included everything from subtle daily occurrences through to her family farm being spared from near-inevitable destruction by a forest fire. When she had finished her stories, the professor, a Muslim, thanked her and commented to the class that, 'This is kind of convincing.'

Afterwards a number of students came to speak with her about what she'd shared. They were really struck by the intimacy of Mariam's described relationship with God and wanted to hear more about it.

Fouad, a colleague of Mariam, told me he went one step further and actively selected classes which would enable him to speak of Jesus. As we sat together on a hillside, overlooking an area described several times in the Bible, he told me how the idea came to him over lunch. Some of his Muslim colleagues had just been attending an elective class in Islamic Studies, open to all students, regardless of their major. Apparently the professor had been sharply critical of Christianity in that day's lesson and had been especially emphatic that the New Testament was corrupt and unreliable. As Fouad sat listening to them vividly recount the content and tone of the lecturer's verbal attack, a plan began to form in his mind.

Ever since stepping on campus, a year previously, Fouad had been careful to foster friendships with students from all religions. Many of his new Muslim friends, he discovered, had never met a Christian before and were genuinely intrigued to begin understanding him and his strange beliefs. He was enjoying the new connections and the many opportunities to discuss Jesus in quiet, interpersonal conversations around campus. But he had also wondered if there was any way he, like Mariam, might speak more publicly of Jesus. Now, as his friends described their frenetically anti-Christian lecturer, he pondered if this might be his opening. He decided right then to enrol for the next available Islamic Studies module.

The class began the next semester with almost fifty Muslim students and, including Fouad, just two Christians.

The first few weeks were uneventful as the professor outlined the history of Islam and some of its key tenets. His style was warmly engaging, even if his content was fairly basic for most of the audience. By the fifth lecture, however, things changed gear. This time the teacher began using various arguments, mostly built around his misinterpretation of an obscure verse from Jeremiah, to explain that the Bible was unreliable. Fouad's moment had come.

He raised his hand and asked whether, as a Christian, he could offer his perspective. The professor, surprised by the intervention, allowed his student to speak. As Fouad began to explain his case the lecturer looked at his watch and explained that time was too tight to dwell on the matter right now. Perhaps, he suggested with a slight edge to his voice, next week's lecture could begin with Fouad giving a fifteen-minute presentation on the reliability of the Christian Scriptures. The tone of his offer suggested an expectation that it would likely be declined. Fouad, however, smiled with gratitude and said that he would be delighted.

His smile wavered throughout the following week as he began to grasp the enormity of what he had taken on. Conversations with Muslim friends were one thing – he could just about handle those – even giving a presentation to his fellow students was just about tolerable. But standing up next to his erudite and learned professor, a man decades his senior and accustomed to publicly and verbally crushing the Christian faith at every opportunity? Perhaps the plan had got out of hand. Yet backing out at this point would be understood as a tacit admission that the Scriptures – and, by extension, the Christian understanding of Jesus – were unreliable. So Fouad spent the week reading, researching and talking with other Christians as he readied his presentation for the following week.

Fouad arrived early and took a seat near the front of the class. When the professor arrived he began, as always, by welcoming the students and introducing the week's topic. Conflicting waves of relief and disappointment washed over Fouad as, for a moment, he thought that his presentation had been forgotten. Before he had a chance to fully process the situation, however, the professor turned to look directly at Fouad, gestured towards him, and said, 'But first, some unfinished business ...'

Fouad rose to his feet, took a deep breath, and with the occasional glance at his notes began to explain carefully how we might decide if a text is accurate or not. The whole class, unaccustomed ever to hearing anyone other than a Muslim publicly speak of their faith, was still and listening. Fouad managed to get through exactly six minutes of his presentation before the professor stepped in and called it to a halt. It could have been a painfully disappointing moment: a sense of opportunity lost. Instead, Fouad felt buoyant. In a nation where Christians can rarely speak publicly of Jesus, he'd been granted a brief window to let a room full of Muslims know that the gospels might not be as unreliable as many Muslim teachers suggest.

In the days that followed, many of Fouad's classmates from Islamic Studies approached him in person as well as through social media. They were intrigued by what they had heard and keen to hear more. As with Mariam, his brief public statements about the Christian faith had unsettled and interested his colleagues. Neither Mariam nor Fouad spoke to their classes for more than a few minutes, but the result was conversations which lasted for many hours and stretched across months. Their tiny pinpricks of public proclamation had opened the door for extensive interpersonal discussion of Jesus and his message. As Vinoth said, 'There is no such thing as a closed or unreachable campus' so long as a follower of Jesus can enrol there as a student.

PERSONAL – BUT NOT PRIVATE

All around the world, Christian students are under pressure to keep their faith private. In most majority-Muslim nations this occurs through a combination of apostasy and blasphemy laws, along with a desire to retain harmony between different groups by minimizing verbal public discord. In Pepper's case, however, it was not legal restrictions or potential punishments which drove her friends to suggest waiting before becoming publicly Christian.[28] It was concern about Pepper's parents. They feared that her mother and father would cut off her financial support and eject her from the home – a common response from Muslim parents whose children leave their faith. Once she had a job, she could support herself and – while their response to her following Jesus might still be painful – it would not leave her homeless and potentially starving.

In the secularized West, the pressure towards a privatized faith often comes from an insistence that one's religion is an intensely personal matter, along with a deeply-ingrained resistance towards any affirmation of knowing *the*

---

[28] I'm told that conversion is theoretically legal in Indonesia but pressuring others to do so is not, and this is frequently used to functionally prohibit evangelism. In Indonesia, a Perkantas staff worker told me, 'It is less about the law and more about the culture'.

truth on such topics. In post-communist Eurasian states (like the one where security services broke up our restaurant-based event) the lingering legacy of state-sponsored atheism blends with governmental fear of free expression to make public articulation of the Christian faith difficult. In other contexts, evangelical voices are marginalized for not being part of the mainstream Eastern Orthodox or Roman Catholic churches. The list goes on. Christians can meet in their own church buildings, perhaps even have conversations with their friends, but when they want to hold an event or even simply to open their mouths to speak of Jesus in a more public way ... well, then they meet resistance, either legally or simply culturally.

It has been this way since the day a bleeding man hung gasping for every breath under the Palestinian sun. He was one of three people killed that day and one of thousands to meet their demise via a form of execution 'specifically designed to be the ultimate insult to personal dignity, the last word in humiliating and dehumanizing treatment ... Executed publicly, situated at a major crossroads or on a well-trafficked artery, devoid of clothing, left to be eaten by birds and beasts, victims of crucifixion were subject to optimal, unmitigated, vicious ridicule.'[29] Marking him out from the others being executed with him was the sign above his head written in three languages, 'Jesus of Nazareth, King of the Jews', and the circle of nail-like thorns jammed into his scalp as an imitation crown.[30] Two mocking gestures intended to communicate that Jesus had failed in his royal pretensions. He and his grand words about his 'kingdom'

[29] Fleming Rutledge, *The Crucifixion: Understanding the Death of Jesus Christ* (Eerdmans, 2017), p.78.
[30] John 19:2; John 19:19.

were being silenced in the most brutal fashion. If only he'd kept his message to himself then this would never have happened.

The official 'King of the Jews' at the time was a Roman puppet, Herod Antipas, who was not from the ancient Davidic royal line. He instead represented a dynasty installed by Julius Caesar's general, Marc Anthony, less than a century earlier. Herod's legitimacy was a source of constant debate for local Jews and when Rome's local representative, Pilate, interrogates Jesus, the focus of his questions is clearly on whether Jesus might be attempting to usurp Herod. It's a fascinating exchange as Pilate recognizes Jesus' claims to kingship – even exclaiming at one point, 'You are a king, then!'[31] – yet hopelessly fails in his attempts to grasp exactly what Jesus means by the word. Theologian Stanley Hauerwas writes:

> Pilate is a state official. He asks the question that is the concern of a state official ... He wants to know if Jesus may be a rival to Herod. One suspects that it would never occur to Pilate that, in reality, Jesus is a rival to Caesar ... He is a king, but his kingship is not that which Pilate can recognize. Pilate's inability to understand the politics of Jesus does not mean Jesus is any less a threat to Rome. Rather, it means that the politics that Jesus represents is a more radical threat to Rome than Rome is capable of recognizing.[32]

---

31 John 18:37.

32 Stanley Hauerwas, *Matthew: Brazos Theological Commentary on the Bible*, (Brazos, 2006), pp.231–232

Pilate's boss, the ruler of the Roman world, was celebrated on ancient coinage as 'the Son of God' whose family had brought 'peace' to the Empire.[33] Jesus was claiming the same about himself and indeed more. He speaks of himself as one who 'came into the world', a hint at his own pre-existence and the fact that he is not simply a rival to the current generation of politicians but the rightful ruler of all reality.[34] Yet for Pilate, Jesus was no more than a possible pretender to the local throne.

Jesus' first followers understood the universality of his claims, though their implications took a little longer to sink in. Within a few years, they were doing something utterly unique in human history: inviting people of all ethnicities and religions to worship their God, and to do so exclusively. Larry Hurtado, an Ancient Historian, says that this was among a cluster of innovative features which made early Christianity unique: until that point, and indeed in most of human history, it was normal for religious beliefs and practices to be stratified along ethnic and tribal boundaries. You might pay homage to the gods of neighbouring cultures and tribes but it was unheard of to have 'an exclusive religious identity, defined entirely by [one's] standing in relation to the one God, and not dependent on, or even connected to, [one's] ethnicity'.[35] Yet the natural outworking of believing Jesus' claims to be the ruler of Herod, Caesar and all people, was to proclaim him to those of every race and religion. He didn't belong to any one segment of people. He was for everyone.

---

33 Michael D. Coogan, *The Oxford History of the Biblical World* (Oxford University Press, 2001) p390, 395.

34 John 18:37.

35 Larry W. Hurtado, *Destroyer of the Gods: Early Christian Distinctiveness in the Roman World* (Baylor University Press, 2016), p.104.

Jesus wasn't simply seen by the early church as the supreme authority figure. He was also one who had the power to transform individuals and communities. Paul, one of the leading figures in first-century Christianity, writes to a community of believers meeting in Rome – a city densely peppered with monuments to Caesar's strength – that 'the gospel ... is the power of God that brings salvation to everyone who believes: first to the Jew, then to the Gentile'.[36] It's a rich little statement – all of humanity is included in the phrases 'Jew' and 'Gentile', and Paul says that by responding to a wonderful verbal declaration (a 'gospel') they will experience God's rescuing power. Later he writes that 'faith comes from hearing'.[37] These are more than soundbites; the first generations of Jesus' followers treated him as a figure of universal relevance who needed to be *spoken* of to outsiders.[38]

When Mariam and Fouad sought opportunity to speak publicly of Jesus, then, their actions demonstrated a conviction that Jesus is indeed *the* king. He is not someone to be kept private. It's very easy for Christians unwittingly to adopt Pilate's perspective on Jesus and treat him as someone of only local significance. Jesus, we reason, can be worshipped by Christians or perhaps even shared within our circle of friends, but we aren't always convinced he

---

36 Romans 1:16.

37 Romans 10:17.

38 The verbal aspect of the early Christian movement was another of its distinctive features. People began following Jesus as they *heard* about him. That's why the biblical book of Acts is crammed full of speeches. Some other ancient Greek and Roman texts also featured speeches as authorial commentary on the action being recorded. Acts differs from this pattern because the speeches are part of the action rather than just reflections on it. The growth of the early church is, in part, the tale of a conversation spreading rapidly across vast distances. See: Ben Witherington III, *The Acts of the Apostles: A Socio-Rhetorical Commentary* (Eerdmans, 1998), p.46.

needs to be proclaimed to everyone. We stick to personal evangelism and forget the public aspect.

Pragmatic concerns often drive this – perhaps the outmoded models of the past no longer work and we declare the whole enterprise dead. Or maybe, as in many Muslim-majority countries, the potentially-devastating consequences of doing so overshadow all else. Yet before we ask, 'Does it work?' or 'Is it possible?', maybe we should instead ask, 'Who is Jesus?' and 'For whom is Jesus?' And then we discover there are no 'Muslim lands' or 'Christian nations', and we realize that the claims of Jesus apply in every context and to all people.

To deny this is tacitly to repudiate both his claims to kingship and also vast swathes of biblical and creedal material, from John's statement that, 'Through him all things were made'[39] to the Nicene Creed's affirmation that he is 'light from light, true God from true God'.[40] He is the source of all reality become one of us and, as such, is not someone about whom we get to decide whether or not to proclaim. He is not the God only of Christians and neither is his message 'the power of salvation' given simply to our own small circle of friends. He is for everyone.

None of this, of course, is to say that we are to proclaim Jesus in a rash and thoughtless manner. Fouad and Miriam found themselves caught between the many legal and cultural obstacles to speaking of Jesus and their own deep conviction of his identity and relevance. They did not respond, however, by simply resigning themselves to the situation. They chose to live in the tension between the

39 John 1:3.

40 Nicene Creed cited in: Alister McGrath (ed.), *The Christian Theology Reader Fifth Edition* (Wiley Blackwell, 2017), p.11.

near-impossibility of proclamation and the fact that Jesus was king of their campus. And when they saw a small opening to speak, they ducked nimbly through it.

THE GIVING TREE

Interestingly, despite the many obstacles faced by campus groups around the world, almost everyone I speak to in IFES tells me that, when they do manage to speak publicly of Jesus, it consistently provokes curiosity from students wanting to find out more. In almost every context the university seems to be a place of spiritual interest. Even in the Middle East, where public proclamation of Jesus is dangerous and often illegal, intense interest is generated by even the simplest of public gestures.

Hazim discovered this when he and his fifteen-strong student group attempted to organize the first ever public Christian outreach in any of his nation's universities. He somehow managed to obtain use of a lecture room on the science campus, located just a few miles down the road from Fouad and Mariam's university. That the administration would grant him permission was a shock in itself; an influential political group (conservative Muslim by orientation) were known to dominate the faculty and Hazim fully expected to have his request to run a Christmas-themed event denied. Instead the group found themselves carefully planning an event which would introduce Muslim colleagues to the message that God has come to us in the person of Jesus.

Some local Christian friends, stand-up comedians with a gift for gently introducing Jesus to sceptical audiences, had agreed to come and speak, while a musical programme of traditional festive music was also planned. All the students in the organizing team had friends planning to attend. Then, just a few days before it was due to happen, Hazim was called into the Dean's office and informed that permission for the room had been rescinded. The Dean was apologetic but explained the decision was rooted in safety concerns for Hazim and his group. Their social media advertising campaign for the event had, they were told, drawn a lot of attention. Many members of the administration were expressing opposition to the event and the Dean feared the muttered misgivings may translate into direct action.

Hazim told me that, on one level, he agreed with the Dean. 'There was', he said, 'absolutely a risk, but it was one we were willing to take.' The Christian students were not perturbed. They came together, prayed and collectively decided to attempt another approach. They asked the university if they could erect a Christmas tree, just six feet tall, in the central quad and have a table from which to distribute gifts. The administration were relieved to find a proposal which honoured the Christian students' festival without providing a platform to messages which could unsettle the university's more conservatively Muslim elements. They were swiftly granted permission to erect the tree for a single day in December.

On the day they all arrived early and erected the tree, covered it with bright lights and colourful bows and then put out three tables with hot chocolate and Christmas cards. Beside the tree they placed a (mostly blank) poster topped by the words, 'Write your wishes for the year'. Pots of coloured pencils lay below for students to take and add in their own words or pictures. Christmas is referred to informally by many local Muslims as 'the tree festival' and the students' display marked out that they were Christians. As content goes, it was as light a public statement as the group could have made. The tree simply said to all walking by, 'Here are some followers of Jesus – they exist in your university'.

As Hazim and his friends stood mixing hot chocolates, members of the administration peering down at them from the office windows which surrounded the quad on all sides, his imagination kept conjuring up unhappy scenes which might unfold. He knew of Christians who had been violently assaulted or stabbed for less than this. At the very least, he thought someone may come and create an emotional scene or overturn the tables in a fit of protest. In the end, none of this happened. Muslim students and staff simply wandered over, took a hot chocolate and card, and then spontaneously asked questions like, 'What is Christmas actually about?' and 'Why are you doing this?' Over the course of the day, Hazim says, his group had over 600 friendly and personal conversations on the meaning of Christmas with teachers and classmates.

Students also came up and wrote on the Christmas wish board. Some wrote about situations with their friends or families, or their own studies. Others just added comments like, 'We love you' and, 'You are kind people'. The Dean even came down and wrote a sentence of thankfulness 'for my Christian brothers'. A member of the university's influential conservative Muslim political group was also heard to say – appreciatively and publicly – that 'these people should be in this college'. I asked Hazim and several of the staff and volunteers from his student movement about the friendly reception they received on campus that day. I wondered if it was anomalous. Each one agreed that they didn't live in an easy context in which to speak of Jesus. But, they added, the culture was changing. The rise of ISIS in the region had caused many in the student generation to reassess Islam. A sizeable proportion of young people had quietly decided that they didn't believe it anymore and were consequently open to tentatively exploring alternatives.[41] Others simply resolved that if they were going to be Muslim then they needed to be the opposite of ISIS. Warmth, welcome and messages of 'We love you, our Christian brothers' were therefore increasingly the order of the day.

Speaking publicly of Jesus, then, is challenging everywhere. But it is always worth doing and usually opens the door to ongoing private discussions. Personal evangelism seems to thrive when accompanied by public proclamation. The two, far from being in tension, actually fuel one another. Most members of this Middle Eastern student movement told me they would love to run something more explicitly explaining the message of Jesus to large audiences in campus. Perhaps a lecture, debate, musical event or simply somebody sharing their own experience of following Jesus. But, for now, they are determined to optimize whatever slight freedoms they can find to engage the interest of people beyond their own small circles of friends. Six hundred conversations and connections as a result of a tree and a few hot chocolates – along with a whole lot of prayer – is a reasonable place to start.

---

[41] Interestingly, the Christian student training camp I attended in this country included much discussion on engaging atheistic students, who – while still legally Muslims – have departed the faith in anything but an official sense. Such students, I was told, have markedly increased in the region since the rise of ISIS.

MISSION LABS

In Indonesia they're starting somewhere else. I witnessed first-hand some of their initial steps towards public proclamation among Muslims when one of my friends, a Perkantas staff member, told me to meet her at 6am outside a bookshop in Jakarta. She told me that she wanted to show me a secret experiment her movement was implementing around the country. 'Mission Labs', as they are dubbed, are effectively the evangelistic research and development facility of Perkantas. A place where students can experiment with speaking publicly of their faith.

The sky was beginning to lighten when her car pulled up. One other staff member and two students were already in the back seat and she pushed the door open for me to get in. We drove through the dense traffic of the city until, after a couple of hours, we began to leave the urban sprawl behind and were increasingly surrounded by single-storey buildings nestled in small courtyards. Palm trees lined our way as we followed a river through a series of villages. Motorcycles buzzed around us as we went.

Eventually, we came to a halt outside a large metal gate and piled out into the street. My friend pushed at the entrance and found it locked. 'We're early,' she told me, 'let's go for a walk.' So we wandered down the river and observed how it was congested with refuse. Plastic bottles, used nappies and sanitary pads, and a whole host of other items lined each side. There was a stench rising up. Downriver some women were washing clothes in the water. My friend asked me, 'Do you know that some of them drink this water? Their children get sick from it.'

We moved on and, as we weaved between the houses, locals smilingly offered nods of welcome, my light skin tone ill-suited to anonymous walkabouts in rural Java. I asked my friend to explain the thinking behind 'Mission Labs'. She said that it began when some staff from Perkantas admitted that they and their students really didn't know how to speak publically about Jesus to Muslims. Yes, she affirmed, there were cultural and sometimes legal or practical barriers to doing any campus-based Christian outreach events. But, along with all the logistical issues, they also had to admit that it was an area in which they lacked experience. They simply didn't know how to do it.

Mission Labs were therefore conceived of as projects where students could undertake practical tasks for the benefit of underprivileged communities and, as they did so, be open about the fact that love for Jesus is their motivation. In the village I visited, the students provided mathematics tutoring for adolescents and literacy lessons for adult women. Lack of education often accompanies and compounds poverty, so Perkantas' students were addressing a vital need. As they began each lesson they would say something like, 'Welcome to the class, we are Christians and we love you because we believe Jesus loves you.' It was not a sermon, but an extremely gentle statement about the One they follow and his attitude towards humanity. In each lesson I observed, the entirely Muslim class responded by smiling in appreciation at this introduction.

For the Christian students, it grew in them a little confidence that maybe their understanding of Jesus could be aired to Muslim audiences without ensuing rancour or discord. Maybe even on campus. When, some months later, I asked Fouad why he thought Jesus wasn't often proclaimed publicly in many Muslim nations, he replied immediately with one word – 'cowardice'. He asserted that the greatest barrier to the proclamation of Jesus is often the timidity of Christians. Perkantas have come to the same conclusion and so they temporarily remove their students from their everyday university setting to experience elsewhere the possibility of speaking with Muslims about Jesus. Their hope is that, as the students return to their dorms and lecture rooms, they might begin imagining new possibilities for their campus.

As we drove back at the end of the day, I told my friend how much I appreciated what they were doing. There was an honesty to admitting confusion as to the way ahead. But, instead of surrendering in the face of their quandary about public proclamation, they chose to take some small steps towards learning how they might speak of Jesus in their overwhelmingly Muslim context. As with Hazim's group and their hundreds of conversations around the Christmas tree, the Indonesian students discovered that – masked beneath the legal restrictions and institutional opposition to speaking about Jesus – there lay a warmth and even an openness in the hearts of many individual Muslims.

SURPRISING OUTCOMES

Christian students in Muslim-majority contexts, then, find it challenging to speak of Jesus beyond their own circle of friends. Legal and practical barriers are ranged all around them. Yet 'difficult' is not a synonym for 'impossible'. Rather than focusing on the numerous obstacles, they instead pray for discernment and courage to observe and seize the opportunities. Consistently they find themselves surprised by what occurs. It would be easy to idealize the bravery of students in these settings, yet – like followers of Jesus in every nation on earth – they struggle with timidity and fear, often with much better grounding for their worries than most of us in less restrictive settings.

Those Muslims who do begin to consider Jesus, however, often find him compelling. Pepper did. Her life was nudged in a new direction by her unsettling dreams. But it was transformed through her conversations with Christian students. Their time together discussing the life and message of Jesus, as well as the books they lent her, redirected the course of her life. As with most Muslims who begin following Jesus after a dream, Pepper's vision wasn't the end of the story but the beginning. It was in the context of friendship with a group of Christian students that she learned a new way of life. The interpersonal element is always vital, whether as a counterpart to dreams or to public proclamation.

Pepper went on to postgraduate study overseas in another majority-Muslim country. Once there, she quietly discarded her hijab and all her new friends assumed she was from a Christian home. She began attending church for the first time and it swiftly became family to her, just as she had experienced with her group of coffee-drinking student friends back in Jakarta. She has even since shared her conversion story with her parents. Her father is vocally unimpressed and would probably have evicted her if she still lived at home. Her mother was quietly sympathetic and is beginning to secretly read about Jesus for herself. Every day she becomes a little more open.

And so, even when law, government, and culture assert that we may not change our views about God, and insist that if you're born into one religion you can never become a follower of Jesus, the King overrules all their decrees and – through small groups of students, often scared and marginalized – he draws individuals and families to himself.

QUESTIONS FOR REFLECTION OR DISCUSSION:

What pressures can you identify in your own life, or in your cultural context, towards keeping Jesus private?

Where is your Christian community strongest in terms of engaging those not following Jesus with his life and message: in public, small group, or interpersonal settings? What practical steps could you take to be more active and effective in the others?

What would a 'Mission Lab' look like in your setting? Sketch out some ideas below.

CHAPTER THREE:
TOMBSTONES AND PAINTINGS

TALES OF PROMOTING JUSTICE
(GUATEMALA AND THE UNITED STATES)

A child climbs the hill. It's not easy as the ground keeps moving beneath him. He pauses every so often to adjust his footing. He's been scrambling up these mounds almost as long as he could walk and instinctively knows when to pause and when to push on ahead. The aim is to close his stubby four-year-old hands around something valuable and take it back down. Not gold or money. But maybe a metal can, a plastic bottle or perhaps a pile of old magazines. Anything for which his family might get a few *centavos* to go towards the week's bread. Reaching the grubby metal chain for which he's been aiming, he carefully pulls it towards him, grips it tightly in his fist and begins making his way back down.

At the foot of the hill he heads back over to his nearby mother. She, too, is rifling through mounds of refuse for items she can sell on to recyclers. He drops his find at her feet and she observes its weight. It's a good discovery – probably discarded from a suburban child's bicycle. The child pauses and sits for a moment. All around him is the sound of bulldozer engines and, above that, the calls of vultures, who constantly patrol the dust-filled sky and fill the branches of the trees that encircle an area locals refer to as 'The Dump'. An enormous trash heap spanning forty acres, The Dump grows bigger each year as the edges subside. Landslides are frequent and deaths usually remain uncounted.

The child lives in a makeshift shack at the edge of The Dump; its pink-painted walls of corrugated iron are pinned into wooden uprights and provide a little privacy in the evenings. Not that the child often chooses to be alone. He is one of thousands, including many other children, who reside in these shed-like homes. He is thankful that his mother chooses to spend her day's money on food and not – as with many of his playmates' parents – on the small packets of white powder young men sell each evening at dusk. Neither he nor his friends have been to school and very few can read. They, and even their parents, have no inkling of the numerous political and business decisions which led to the creation of The Dump. You would only draw blank stares if you asked these kids about the rotting stench which constantly fills the air; they don't even notice it. They've never known anything else.[42]

Just five miles away, the scene couldn't be more different. Streams of smiling students in brightly-coloured clothing pass one another on clean concrete walkways lined by lush green grass. Their backpacks are full of books on every imaginable subject, from architecture and sociology to biology and linguistics. Palm trees, surrounded by vibrant

---

[42] This chapter's opening three paragraphs are an imaginative blending of scenes described to me by Guatemalans who have visited or worked in The Dump, along with my own observations and details drawn from this article: Benjamin Reeves, 'The Humanitarian Crisis in Guatemala City's Immense Garbage Dump', *Vice*, 25 March 2014, https://www.vice.com/en_us/article/vdpbxm/the-basurero-is-burning-life-at-the-gates-of-hell-in-guatemala-city (Accessed 28 March 2019).

orange and pink flowers, provide shade above the many clusters of circular benches where everyone congregates for conversation between lectures.

Yet, even here at the prestigious Universidad de San Carlos de Guatemala, whispers of pain and injustice are unavoidable. You see it most clearly in the artwork. It is impossible to turn a corner on campus without being confronted by an enormous mural consuming an entire wall. Most show the faces of revolutionary figures like Che Guevara or depict the suffering of Guatemalan peasants under the landowning classes. A sense of struggle shines through each one.

One particularly striking painting takes up the entire side of a building and depicts a mint green hooded figure, with a Universidad de San Carlos crest for a face, cracking a whip explosively on the ground. Above, in yellow, are written the condemnatory words, 'Students, I expect you will graduate to become ...' The sentence is then finished below, at the point of the whip's impact, with the word 'exploiters'. It's both pessimistic but also, one local Christian leader tells me, almost prophetic: many of the students will graduate from university to become perpetuators of the injustice and corruption which created and sustains The Dump. They, like the figure in this painting, will crack the whip.

On this day, however, much smaller works of art are absorbing the attention of passers-by. Wooden easels, placed a metre apart, run down both sides of the campus' main walkway. Each displays a student photograph or painting on the theme of 'Justice and Sexuality' along with a short, printed explanation by the artist of their work. Around the images mill students in grey T-shirts who strike up conversations with those who pause to look. On the back of their T-shirts is printed a logo reading, in Spanish, 'Festival of Art for Life'. On the front of each one is a Bible verse. Mine reads: 'I have come that they may have life, and have it to the full'.[43]

The Festival of Art is organized by Grupo Evangélico Universitario de Guatemala (GEU), the Guatemalan IFES student movement, and over the course of two days it will engage hundreds of students. Jhonny Corado, one of the driving forces behind the Festival, told me that justice tends to be an issue more prevalent in campus murals than in the career-focused minds of most Universidad de San Carlos students. He wanted to provoke the students, Christian or otherwise, to see the needs in their country and begin to consider their response. They are the elite of the country and the ones who will shape its future.

To achieve this aim, GEU opened the creative side of the festival to all students and societies who might wish to participate. Most of the pictures lining the pathway are not by Christians, but they raise questions of hope, sexual identity, beauty and much else besides. Ruth Rodas, a local GEU staff worker, told me that her favourite picture was a postcard-sized watercolour of a Mayan woman carrying a baby on her back. Beneath were written the words, 'Every person is born with hope, it is inside us that we might keep it'. The artist was a student they had never met until she submitted her art.

The students and staff of GEU, as they planned the week, considered carefully how they would voice a Christian perspective into its events. One outcome of this discussion

---

43 John 10:10.

was a set of two paintings, created collectively by three people. The first, 'A Ruined Plan', depicts a dark scene with economically-enslaved farmers – as well as office workers at their desks – all chained to the university library, in which are seated several faceless suited men. These figures represent the small cartel of families who have controlled all of Guatemala, from education and banking to politics and entertainment, for decades. Between the university building and the sky is a severed rope. It is an image of our fallen world, cut adrift from God and with humans exploiting and abusing one another.

The second image shows the same university building surrounded by flourishing fields, and the chains, along with those holding them, have been removed. A pair of hands, representing the action of God through Christ in the world, is tying the broken rope back together. Six figures dressed in the clothing of various professions, including a doctor in a white coat and an engineer carrying blueprints, are surrounded by paper aeroplanes flying out to the renewed environment around them. It is an image of a people reconnected with God, and a people and land refreshed as a result.

These two paintings face each other at the end of the walkway and, from my observations, seem to generate more conversation than any other piece of art. The murals may have dominated the campus in size, but it was the art of GEU and their friends which was grabbing the imagination of students this day.

TORN PHOTOS AND BROKEN IMAGES

Just down from the easels in The Igloo, a circular several-hundred-seater auditorium sunk into the ground beneath a white and blue concrete dome, the questions raised in the paintings are being explored through other media. From 10am until 10pm every day, a series of dramatic and musical performances, dance pieces and spoken word acts are woven around a series of TED-style talks from GEU staff and collaborators outlining a biblically-informed view of ecology, sexuality, human flourishing and economic oppression. The talks and discussions all include at least one Christian speaker but the other performances have – just like the paintings – been submitted by a broader segment of students from across campus.

One highpoint of the festival is a public dialogue between four people: a Marxist professor, a feminist activist, a gay visual artist and an evangelical theologian. These four diverse characters, spread across a large sofa and a lone armchair, engage one another's viewpoints with thoughtfulness and respect. Differences are not avoided but instead aired and dealt with directly. Otto Enriquez, a decades-long supporter and former board member of GEU, told me afterwards how enthused he was that so many students had now seen that the Christian faith offers a viable alternative to the other philosophies vying for students' minds.

Not everybody, however, was so captivated. One student, seemingly a professing Christian, became so agitated by it all that he went outside and stormed GEU's art exhibition. He proceeded to walk away with one of the pictures that explored sexual identity, before ripping it to shreds and scattering the pieces on the pavement as he shouted loudly that there was no place for LGBTQI+ students in Universidad de San Carlos de Guatemala.

All this occurred, ironically, at the exact moment in the dialogue that Olber Martinez, of Movimiento Universitario Cristiano (MUC; IFES El Salvador), was on The Igloo's stage beside gay visual artist Juan Pensamiento Velasco, calmly debating sexuality and human flourishing. The contrast in approaches, each occurring just fifty metres apart, could not be more vivid: one was hostile and aggressive, the other respectful and dialogical. It seemed inconceivable to our iconoclastic intruder that the latter could occur without terrible compromise. Yet who could read the New Testament stories of Jesus, so stuffed full of his interaction with all kinds of people, and conclude that he – like Olber – would not be on the stage talking with Juan Pensamiento Velasco. Conversation was not a synonym for compromise in Jesus' mind.

It's not only in Guatemala that Christians struggle with social engagement. Michelle Higgins experienced something similar when she spoke at the Urbana student missions conference, co-hosted by InterVarsity Christian Fellowship (IVCF) in St Louis, USA.[44] She was speaking at a tense time in her nation's history. The previous year an unarmed African American teenager, Michael Brown, had died in the street after being pierced by six bullets from a police officer's gun. Mass protests ensued and were reported to have been met with tear gas and rubber

---

44 IVCF USA co-hosts Urbana with IVCF Canada and GBU Canada.

bullets from members of the same police force which killed Brown.[45] Amnesty International released a scathing report of the military-style suppression of protest and Navi Pillay, the South African-born United Nations Commissioner for Human Rights, condemned 'the excessive use of force by the police' which she said caused her to think 'that there are many parts of the United States where apartheid is flourishing'.[46]

Brown's death, which occurred in the town of Ferguson – just eleven miles from where Higgins was speaking – had come to encapsulate a growing sense that an increasingly militarized police force was tacitly permitted to use excessive (and often lethal) force against African Americans. The entire justice system, from policing through to the courts, seemed stacked against black Americans. Active within the Ferguson protests had been an informal organization called Black Lives Matter. It had begun two years previously as a social media hashtag – #BlackLivesMatter – after the individual who killed another unarmed African American teenager, Trayvon Martin, was also controversially acquitted. The perceived unwillingness to hold white people to account for apparently unjust slayings of African Americans meant that there was a felt need to affirm that black lives matter *just as much* as everyone else's. Hence the slogan.

---

45 See: Francesca Trianni 'Watch: Protesters Hit With Tear Gas and Rubber Bullets During Ferguson Unrest', *Time*, 14 August 2014, http://time.com/3111829/ferguson-tear-gas-rubber-bullets-protests/ (Accessed 28 March 2019); Jon Swaine 'St Louis police chief says only criminals were teargassed at Ferguson protests', *The Guardian*, 17 November 2014, https://www.theguardian.com/us-news/2014/nov/17/st-louis-police-chief-denies-teargas-rubber-bullets-ferguson (Accessed 28 March 2019).

46 'On the Streets of America: Human Rights Abuses in Ferguson', *Amnesty International* (Amnesty International: 2014), p.6.

The national statistics tell a grim story: in the US, as a whole, African Americans are five times more likely to be incarcerated than whites.[47] There seems to be a tendency on the part of law enforcement and the judiciary to be more lenient and understanding towards white people than African Americans. White and African Americans, for example, use drugs at almost exactly the same rates but the latter are imprisoned six times as often for such offences. A criminal conviction for drugs can destroy an individual's future work prospects. This is literally doubly-so for African Americans – research shows that potential employers are twice as likely to offer a white ex-offender a second chance than an African American one. And these are just the figures in relation to justice and law enforcement, not to mention the many other areas of society where similar stories could be told. As a community, they are pushed down and kept down by the system.

Michelle Higgins, asked to speak – at a time and place so close to Ferguson – about how oppressed people respond to injustice, could hardly avoid the matter. Her daily work, as co-founder and director of 'a coalition of Christian activists pursuing the biblical call to action in the public sphere' called Faith for Justice, was always to do the opposite.[48] She gave a passionate and lyrical address to the crowd of 15,000 who filled The Dome, a sports stadium and conference centre which hosts Urbana every three years. Her message, interwoven throughout with references to

---

47 This and all other statistics in this paragraph are taken from: 'Criminal Justice Factsheet', NAACP, https://www.naacp.org/criminal-justice-fact-sheet/ (Accessed 28 March 2019).

48 'Who We Are', *Faith for Justice*, https://www.faithforjustice.org/who-we-are/ (Accessed 28 March 2019).

Scriptural themes, dissected US history and highlighted the way African Americans, indigenous peoples and even Japanese Americans – over 110,000 of whom had been forced into concentration camps during the Second World War – had been victims of a 'white is right' mentality, which the evangelical church often tacitly endorses.

She told the students:

> Black Lives Matter is not a mission of hate. It is not a mission to bring about incredible anti-Christian values and reforms to the world. Black Lives Matter is a movement on a mission in the truth of God … You don't get to decide what human dignity is, or who gets it, or who gets access to it … We have all of the techniques, all of the people that we need to eliminate both racial- and class-based injustice on this continent. We have all we need, except the will to do it.

It wasn't long before many evangelical corners of the Internet exploded in response to Higgins' words. On the official Urbana blog the following day many of the comments were cutting.[49] One student wrote, 'A political movement is not why people are coming to Urbana. This conversation is not about Jesus but an agenda'. Another said, 'This statement and her comments [incite] riots and promote hatred towards police officers and white people'. Another reader, presumably the parent of a student participant, said, 'We feel cheated by sending our children to such a conference. Everything else you try to do in the conference just got devalued and became questionable!' A frequent theme

---

49 All quotes in this paragraph taken from the comments section of: 'Black Lives Matter: Going Deeper', *Urbana*, 29 December 2015, https://urbana.org/blog/black-lives-matter-going-deeper (Accessed 28 March 2019).

of commenters was that 'Jesus' primary concern was not social justice but salvation' and 'what really matters is … eternal salvation for all'.

Bloggers and columnists across the web produced a stream of articles dissecting and critiquing Higgins' words. Many were upset that IVCF had seemingly chosen to align itself with a movement, Black Lives Matter, whose supporters sometimes use incautious language about police officers. Others were concerned about Higgins' criticism of evangelicals as caring about abortion to the exclusion of all other justice issues, including racial justice and the adoption crisis. InterVarsity clarified its own position on the last day of the conference, with a statement:

> *We chose to address #BlackLivesMatter at Urbana … InterVarsity's Student Missions Conference, because it is a language and experience of many college students. Many black InterVarsity staff and students report that they are physically and emotionally at risk in their communities and on campus. About one-half of those at Urbana are people of color, including more than 1,200 black participants. InterVarsity chose to participate in this conversation because we believe that Christians have something distinctive to contribute in order to advance the gospel.*
>
> *InterVarsity does not endorse everything attributed to #BlackLivesMatter. For instance, we reject any call to attack or dehumanize police. But – using the language of Francis Schaeffer and Chuck Colson – we are co-belligerents with a movement with which we sometimes disagree because we believe it is important*

to affirm that God created our black brothers and sisters. They bear his image. They deserve safety, dignity and respect. InterVarsity believes all lives are sacred – born and unborn …

We see racial reconciliation as an expression of the gospel (e.g. Ephesians 2:14–18), and as an important practice in preparation for global missions. The need for reconciliation is obvious in the Middle East and other global mission fields. It is just as obvious in the United States. InterVarsity has been involved in this conversation for decades. We believe it is important to stand alongside our black brothers and sisters.

The statement clarified potential misunderstandings about IVCF's stance towards Black Lives Matter and the issue of abortion. But it expressed no sympathy for the idea that personal salvation should be their only focus. They, like the students of GEU at Universidad de San Carlos de Guatemala, were unflinching in their insistence that a missional Christian movement must be actively involved in the key justice conversations of their culture. Silence on these matters doesn't 'say nothing'; it instead shouts loudly that we neither care nor consider it a priority for followers of Jesus.

TOUCHABLE SPIRITUALITY

Engagement in our context is a prerogative modelled for us by Jesus. Many years before IVCF or GEU were born, on a chilly morning by the water, Jesus sat with his knees pressed down into the stony sand of the beach.[50] He gripped the

---

50 The following beach scene is drawn from John 21:1–14 – my thanks to Ellis Potter for first highlighting to me the striking nature of this scene.

smooth wood of a stick and pulled it from the fire. Using the fingertips of his right hand he carefully removed the skewered fish and tore it into two pieces. He then stretched forward and held a piece out for his friend to take. Lifting the other half to his mouth, he crushed his teeth down on it and began to chew. It tasted delicious.

Jesus' friends also ate the food. What else do you do when your recently-deceased friend offers to cook breakfast? But the atmosphere was uncomfortable. Nobody spoke. Partly, perhaps, it was that Jesus was supposed to be dead. But this was the third time they'd seen him alive since the chaos of his execution. The shock they felt was now no longer only at *seeing* him. Something new was occurring in this encounter – Jesus was now doing a number of painfully mundane everyday things; eating, sitting, cooking, just hanging out on the beach.

Everybody has an idea of what happens to you after death: maybe you come back as a ghost, perhaps you travel to the spirit realm or your soul finds rest and peace in another dimension, or it could be that you become one with the universe. Jesus, though, had died a real death – heart failure, cessation of brain activity, *rigor mortis*, the whole deal – and so to look at Jesus in the days after his resurrection was to glimpse a unique snapshot of life beyond the grave. And, well, it looked a lot more physical than many of us might expect.

Paul, reflecting on Jesus' resurrection a few years later, writes that God one day 'will transform our lowly bodies so that they will be like his glorious body'.[51] Our destiny, in other words, is as physical as the morning a sandy-footed

---

51 Philippians 3:21.

Jesus spent knocking up a hearty meal for his friends. It is not a future as disembodied spirits, but one where friendship, food and places continue to be important. C.S. Lewis, in his book *The Great Divorce*, describes people in the new earth pricking their feet on blades of grass which feel 'hard as diamonds' because the future is *more* (not *less*) solid than our present.[52]

Christian spirituality is not, then, about escape from our physical existence, though it certainly embraces the non-material dimensions of reality as fully as those we can touch or measure. We worship, after all, the uncreated source of all matter. But we do this – both now and in the future – as physical beings in a material world surrounded by objects and people unique to each specific local setting.

This came home to me quite powerfully recently as I sat in the coffee room of my local bookshop reading slowly through John's Gospel to trace the story which led up to Jesus' piscine barbeque. On my way I'd passed the store's 'Spirituality' and 'Personal Development' sections and had paused to flick through their pages. The focus of each one seemed to be on the individual's emotional or relational well-being. Spiritual flourishing appeared to be about an inner calm, insulated from the world around.

John's narrative, however, seemed to convey very different ideas: his tale hasn't even passed its second chapter before Jesus is wreaking havoc at his nation's main worship venue by flipping over furniture and sending people fleeing for the exits in fear over his protest at the easy relationship between the religious establishment and exploitative financial practices. The Temple had become a commercial enterprise. Jesus calls it

---

52 C.S. Lewis, *The Great Divorce* (Collins, 1982), p.30.

'a market', with its intended purpose crowded out by dubious financiers aiming to convert religion into a business.[53]

Soon after, Jesus hits the borderlands to spend a few days befriending his nation's traditional ethnic antagonists, the Samaritans. Even then he doesn't approach local leaders but rather a woman isolated from her community – she becomes the one through whom he engages the whole village. His friends are stunned into silence by what they witness. Their teacher has crossed racial barriers and ignored cultural prohibitions on speaking alone with women.

When Jesus returns home, he keeps spending time with the oddballs around him. In a culture where sickness was assumed to be the result of personal sin, and national sin was seen as the cause of the hated Roman occupation, those suffering with illness were often viewed with contempt. They were seen as part of the cause of the Romans' presence. Their sin was seen to have brought all this on Israel. Jesus' healing miracles were therefore a means of reintegrating these distrusted fringe characters into everyday life.

I was still less than a third of my way into John's Gospel when I read of a woman – probably naked at the time – who is seized literally halfway through a sexual encounter and dragged from the bedroom to the city centre where an angry crowd stands, rocks tightly gripped in their white-knuckled fists, ready to shred her to pieces for her infidelities. The man she slept with? He's allowed to slip away quietly. It's a world where women are killed for their lusts and men are politely excused. Jesus is having none of it. He stands down the entire crowd with a single, penetrating sentence which sends everyone slinking away.

---

53 John 2:14–16.

We could carry on picking examples of the things Jesus does in John's Gospel. It provides such a rich portrait of a man fully engaged with his surroundings and consistently unsettling others by the way he acts and the people with whom he chooses to interact. And this is just his *deeds* in the opening sections of one gospel – it isn't even touching on his extended blocks of teaching or any of the other three gospel narratives. Jesus, in the end, wasn't killed only for his messianic claims or even his divine ones. He was killed because, as he made those claims, he behaved and spoke in a way which unsettled many and caused them to wish he was dead.

The early church understood this very clearly. Sociologist and historian Rodney Stark, a noted researcher of ancient Christianity, says that the early Jesus movement grew – in part – as a result of how it treated abandoned children and vulnerable women, its compassionate response to natural disasters, and the sense of family it provided to the displaced.[54] The priorities and character of Jesus shone through their actions. Paul calls the church 'the body of Christ',[55] and the Christian community is to be his physical presence in the world. It is therefore a denial of its own identity when the church withdraws from engagement with the concrete challenges and injustices of its specific context.

The wisdom of IVCF's choice to use the language of the Black Lives Matter movement may be open to debate. But the imperative to speak and act on issues of injustice is not simply an optional extra for followers of Jesus: it is

---

54 See: Rodney Stark, *The Rise of Christianity: How the Obscure, Marginal Jesus Movement Became the Dominant Religious Force in the Western World in a Few Centuries* (HarperCollins, 1997), especially chapters five and seven.

55 1 Corinthians 12:27.

the natural outcome of being aligned with someone whose actions, both before his death and after his resurrection, were physical ones which engaged his entire context. He behaved and spoke in ways which challenged the surrounding culture's settled approaches to economics, race and ethnicity, violence, gender and even religion. Both IVCF and GEU were following his example as they spoke into the hottest conversations of their own contexts.

In the contemporary Americas, where injustice and racial tension have been part of the cultural fabric since – at the very latest – the day Christopher Columbus spearheaded the European takeover of the region by spending his first few hours in the 'New World' picking out six locals he could export back home as a gift for the King of Spain.[56] One would expect the church to have long been emulating the example of Jesus and his earliest followers by wading knee-deep into the injustice and pain around them. Yet this is often not the case.

Despite the number of evangelicals in Guatemala leaping from one per cent to forty per cent of the population over the past one hundred years, they have frequently left the nation's social problems untouched.[57] The nation's first evangelical president, Efrain Ríos Montt, oversaw a regime which 'committed unspeakable atrocities, including massacres of indigenous communities'.[58] When I asked David Bahena, the IFES Regional Secretary for Latin America, why he thought the evangelical numerical

---

56 See: Christopher Columbus, *The Four Voyages* (Penguin, 1969), p.56; or look into any recent history of Columbus' voyages.

57 Todd Hartch, *The Rebirth of Latin American Christianity* (Oxford University Press, 2014), p.30.

58 Hartch, *The Rebirth of Latin American Christianity*, p.61.

explosion in Latin America wasn't transforming society, he replied that there is a tendency for many churches to teach only about an individual's walk with God or their familial relationships. The call to act or to speak in wider society is left largely untouched. Many Latin American evangelicals, he said, simply wouldn't see addressing poverty or the oppression of ethnic minorities as an essential outworking of their faith.

It's not much different in the United States. Walk into almost any Christian bookshop and you'll find a host of volumes on being a better spouse or parent, along with a range of works on prayer and sexual purity. But there's usually almost nothing on racial reconciliation, peace-making or poverty relief.[59] These are fringe interests for the church. The same indifference is evident if you visit a typical US church on a Sunday morning. The chances are that most faces gathered will be of a similar hue. You don't, in fact, even need to visit. Go to most US church websites and you may see it decorated with stock photos of racially diverse folk flashing relaxed smiles at one another, but click on the leadership team photos and you'll likely find just one ethnic group runs it all. Fifty years after the formal end of segregation, eighty per cent of all churches are still formed almost entirely from a single ethnic group.[60] Racism is a huge issue in the United States, but the church is too often – at best – inert on the matter, and more frequently simply mirroring the wider culture.

---

59 A notable exception are the books published by InterVarsity Press (IVP), the publishing arm of IVCF.

60 Michael Lipka, 'Many U.S. congregations are still racially segregated, but things are changing', *Pew Research Center*, 8 December 2014, http://www.pewresearch.org/fact-tank/2014/12/08/many-u-s-congregations-are-still-racially-segregated-but-things-are-changing-2/ (Accessed 28 March 2019).

GEU's justice-oriented Festival of Art, along with IVCF's bold public commitment to engaging racial tensions in the United States, is therefore unusual among the evangelical scene of the Americas. When I first encountered these movements, I was intrigued by what made them so different. I began an investigation by sending emails and continued it through innumerable Skype conversations with local students and staff from each movement, until – before I knew it – I found myself staring into the darkness of an open grave on the outskirts of Guatemala City. It was here that I began to discover how GEU had become unique.

TOMBSTONE DISCIPLESHIP

I say 'grave', but it looked more like an exceptionally deep storage locker – a long, thin cuboid with concrete walls and just enough space to neatly slide and store an adult's corpse. This snug burial chamber was set into a towering wall on which lay, spaced as neatly as boxes on an Excel spreadsheet, a grid – nine rows by fifty-three columns – of granite, marble and plaster plaques each measuring around one foot up by two feet across. The crumbling surface of the structure, both its paintwork and core materials, suggested decades of neglect. Yet most of the inscriptions were from within just the last ten years.

'The poor don't rest in peace in Guatemala'. Teddy Torres, my guide for the afternoon, broke the silence. He explained to me that these were graves for members of the very poorest families. Their relatives scraped together all the *quetzals* they could to pay the $24 rent for the burial and first six years of internment.[61] When the money for renewal fees runs out, as it usually does at some point, the authorities smash open the placard, pull the body out and place it in a bin along with bags of everyday rubbish. Dozens of these holes pepper each of the innumerable similar walls scattered throughout the Guatemala City General Cemetery.

Opposite this particular wall, separated only by a thin cracked walkway, is a towering pyramid constructed of smooth greyish-white stone. Each corner of this immaculate edifice features a human figure in traditional ancient Egyptian dress, arms crossed over its chest, staring down at the ground. An enormous face, complete with pharaonic headdress stares unblinkingly ahead from the structure's roof. Just beneath this visage lies the pyramid's vast wooden door, topped by a brass engraving of an eagle, which seals the entrance to a spacious tomb. The one body lying within belonged to someone from one of a handful of families who have controlled Guatemala for over a century. With no sense of irony she chose to be interred in an ostentatious building designed to pay tribute to the famously slave-driving dynasties of the ancient Nile kingdom. All this just a few feet away from where the serfs of the economic system which her family regulates have their own corpses yanked out and trashed every year for want of a few *quetzals*.

Every couple of years, Teddy brings a group of new GEU students to stand on this exact spot and contemplate what they see. It is the first stop on a walking tour outlining 'four

---

61 This seems to be the figure (give or take a dollar) cited by locals and also by most news reports, such as: David Gonzalez, 'In Guatemala, Exhuming Children to Make Room for Death', *The New York Times*, 31 July 2015 https://lens.blogs.nytimes.com/2015/07/31/in-guatemala-exhuming-children-to-make-room-for-death/ (Accessed 28 March 2019).

collective wounds' which have injured Guatemala and is a part of what he calls his 'Ministry of Memory'. The pyramid and the crumbling wall represent the 'economic wound' – the staggering levels of inequality and exploitation that have grown up in the country over the past few centuries. Other stops include a sacred Mayan site hidden between the graves and desecrated by European colonialists. It symbolizes the 'ethnic wound' of interracial division. The 'religious wound' of conflict between Protestants and Catholics and the 'political wound' of the various dictatorial regimes and disastrous US interventions into national governance are also discussed at length. The whole tour finishes on a hill overlooking The Dump. For most students, coming from more comfortable family backgrounds, witnessing this kind of deprivation first hand is shocking.

GEU sends its students on this tour to help them understand the context in which they live. The visit to the cemetery and The Dump is, in fact, one of two such outings the GEU group in Guatemala City arranges for its freshmen. The other is a guided survey of the many campus murals, specially designed to help students make sense of the history and values of the campus where they are studying. Ruth Rodas, an art history graduate and GEU staff member, told me that she formulated this tour – along with an accompanying illustrated guidebook – to be part of the way they help students grow as followers of Jesus.

But these tours are not the only important element in GEU's discipleship of students. GEU has a stunning track record of sending its graduates into justice ministries, including former GEU General Secretaries Vinicio Zuquino – now tackling violence against women with the

CAMPUS LIGHTS

International Justice Mission – and Israel Ortiz, whose Ezra Centre seeks to provide church leaders with a biblical and holistic approach to making justice a part of their teaching and praxis. I made a point of asking each GEU student, staff member and graduate what had awakened this priority in them. Surprisingly, none of them pointed primarily to the tours of graveyards, slums and murals; instead they mentioned studying the New Testament, especially the life and teaching of Jesus, as the pivotal aspect in their wanting to engage their campus and the wider needs of the country. Seeing his attitude to the poor, the ethnically 'other' and the bodies and lives of people undeserving of his love, grew in them a desire to go and be the body of Christ in Guatemala.

Staff of GEU invite all their new members to join small groups which meet across campus. The focus of these gatherings, which normally max out at three or four students, is to look at New Testament passages together, especially the four gospels. The groups seek to understand what they read and then to apply it to their own lives, as well to the national and campus culture. Alongside the small groups, GEU staff have designed a series of five modules which they encourage each student to undertake. These include intensives on inductive Bible study, how to lead a small group, evangelism, apologetics and biblical counselling. Students can study the modules, which are intended to provide them with a basic set of skills and understanding for work among students, as seminar tracks at national conferences, as well as when they are delivered locally. Advanced courses on things like hermeneutics (biblical interpretation) and social work are also available. In all these there is a focus on allowing the biblical text to guide their understanding of the topic at hand.

The campus tours and graveyard visits are not designed to replace this immersion in the Scriptures. They are, instead, intended to provide a reference point for students as they seek to apply what they are reading and discussing. It helps students read the New Testament in the context, not only of their own personal spiritual experience, but also of the city and campus in which they find themselves. By incorporating concrete engagement with their physical surroundings into the *formación* of newcomers, they ensure that students' wrestling with Jesus' life and ethical imperatives has, as one of its natural consequences, engagement with both campus and wider culture. They begin to ponder whether part of following Jesus implies helping to heal the ethnic, religious, political and economic wounds around them.

The development of bold public events like the Festival of Art is, then, rooted in something much quieter and less visible than a theatrical performance or an art exhibition: the gathering of small groups of students to contemplate Jesus and the Scriptures, along with working to understand the context in which they find themselves. An orientation towards justice is not something we can glue on artificially through the implementation of flashy projects; it requires a consistent focus on Jesus and his teaching, as well as a proactive effort to relate this thoughtfully to the questions and challenges of the context in which we find ourselves.

Big events, of course, can play a part in helping grow this focus. GEU staff members told me that the Festival of Art helped their students refocus on what it means to live and speak for Jesus amidst the many challenges of life in contemporary Guatemala. There is clearly discipleship value in conferences and large gatherings, but their effectiveness is hindered if the remainder of the community's life is inward-focused and marginalizes the relevance of biblical teaching for all of life, and not just for our own individual relationships with God. This is true in the city where the graves of the poor are smashed open in the shadow of a wealthy woman's pyramid tomb. It is equally as relevant in the racially divided context of the United States, where Thurston Benns, an IVCF staff worker, was crying as he listened to Michelle Higgins give her controversial address at Urbana.

COMMUNITY LIFE MATTERS

Thurston's tears came not because anything Michelle said was new or unexpected, but rather, because the struggles of African American believers like himself were being framed biblically in a compelling message delivered to a large and diverse audience. Thurston says that there is a tendency on the part of many in his country, especially – though by no means limited to – white Americans, to cherish racial 'colour-blindness' as a virtue. This is often well-intentioned: folk regularly assume that not acknowledging the differences, unique experiences and varied daily challenges of other cultural and ethnic groups is a means of reducing racial tensions. 'We're all equal' is confused with 'we're all the same'. Thurston says that one of the first things which attracted him to IVCF was that they *did* acknowledge difference. They seemed comfortable discussing how the White, Black, Asian, Latino, Native and other American experiences all differ and what this implies for following Jesus today.

Thurston told me that he thought the movement was able to make such a bold statement through Michelle Higgins precisely because racial reconciliation is pursued at every level of the organization. Her message was an echo of what occurs from dormitory-based small groups through to executive appointments. If you take a glance at the current IVCF national Executive Team, for example, you'll see people of Chinese, Jewish, Indian, African and East European ancestry. Greg Jao, Senior Assistant to the President of IVCF, commented to me recently that four of the six-strong national leadership team are descendants of recent immigrants or historically-enslaved peoples. Take it down to campus level and over fifty per cent of students – and almost a third of staff – are non-white. This affects the dynamic of the whole movement.

I asked Greg why he thought this situation – so distinct from the racially homogenous church staff photos I kept encountering on American church websites – had arisen. He replied by telling me that IVCF has never been a mono-racial organization and always took a stand against segregation even as far back as the 1940s.[62] But racial reconciliation has become an increasingly unavoidable issue in recent decades because, alongside historical and wider cultural factors, the campus context itself is now so diverse. Studies show that under-eighteens will be majority non-white in the United

---

[62] Even in the 1940s, when the movement was still getting going and much of the USA was still forcibly segregated – often with the churches' tacit (or explicit) support – IVCF founder Stacey Woods was standing up to Christians who wanted Bible studies streamed along racial lines. He also had the movement's magazine, *His*, publish articles urging evangelicals to apply the gospel to the nation's racial divides. Woods was, his biographer says, a 'fearless proponent of integration long before that became acceptable'. A commitment to racial integration, then, has always been there, though the early leadership was mainly white. Jao told me that this emphasis on racial reconciliation grew over time, then peaked in the 1970s before receding, resurfacing again as a consistent focus of the movement from the mid-1980s onwards. See: A. Donald MacLeod, *C. Stacey Woods and the Evangelical Rediscovery of the University*, pp.112–114.

States by 2020.[63] Inter-ethnicity is simply the lived reality of today's generations of students. This, Greg says, is one of the things Michelle Higgins' critics – often a generation or two removed from most undergraduates – failed to grasp: her message at Urbana was expressive not only of IVCF's own internal diversity, but also of the changing university context. Black Lives Matter was relevant because many IVCF chapters had been surrounded by racial tensions on campus all year round.

When I asked Thurston what practices he thought helped IVCF cultivate and maintain their inter-ethnic nature, he told me he thought it helped that they had four national departments each dedicated to developing ministry among Black, Latino, Native and Asian American students respectively. But it also, he said, grew out of things done at the local level. Every IVCF chapter in his region, for example, has at least one teaching series – often accompanied by small group studies – on the topic each academic year.[64] This willingness to deal with race in the core gatherings of the community avoids it being seen as a niche interest and keeps the matter in the consciousness of each new intake of students.

But, Thurston says, IVCF go beyond just good preaching and teaching. They also proactively invest in and develop leaders from all ethnic groups, and staff aim consciously to resist their natural default towards favouring those from

---

63 William H. Frey, 'The US will become "minority white" in 2045, Census projects', *Brookings*, 14 March 2018, https://www.brookings.edu/blog/the-avenue/2018/03/14/the-us-will-become-minority-white-in-2045-census-projects/ (Accessed 28 March 2019).

64 These studies are sometimes based on: Sarah Shin, *Beyond Colorblind: Redeeming Our Ethnic Journey* (IVP, 2017).

within their own cultural or ethnic group. Thurston himself was taken under the wing of his white staff workers who, he says, made 'intentional and costly sacrifices' in supporting black students on campus, and showed them that their 'ethnic-specific ministry mattered, not only to them, but to InterVarsity and to God' – and later, while pursuing graduate studies in theology, was approached and invited by a Chinese American man to become staff, first voluntarily and later salaried.[65]

Thurston told me that, zooming down even from the level of meeting topics and recruitment policies, IVCF make a point of helping students process their own ethnic identity in the light of Scripture. One way they do this in his area, he told me, is through something called Ethnic Lounges, which occur at IVCF's annual Regional Camp in the beautiful valley-based Rockbridge Campsite. These are spaces where students can come together with others of similar race or ethnicity and discuss their experiences and challenges. The White Lounge, Black Lounge, Asian Lounge and Biracial Lounge were some of the options.

In the Black Lounge, most students will tend to be enrolled at majority-white institutions and are therefore usually a minority in both their classes and also their IVCF chapter. They find it very freeing to be able to let their guard down and exchange stories. Thurston says that, because of the socio-economic background of many African American students, they can often be one of the first people from their family to go to university, and so many feel pressure to focus

65 'Thurston Benns & Charlene Brown', *TwentyOneHundred Productions,* 8 May 2015, https://2100.intervarsity.org/resources/thurston-benns-charlene-brown (Accessed 28 March 2019).

mainly on activities which will further their professional prospects. Thurston often encourages them also to consider serving in leadership positions within their IVCF campus group, and even to put themselves forward for this if they feel that the door is not already swinging open to them. Most African American students seem to find the lounge an enjoyable and energizing experience.

Not everyone feels the same way about ethnic lounges. At least, not initially: one of Thurston's colleagues, a white staff worker called Blake Phillips, says that he rolled his eyes the first time he – as a student – heard there was a White Lounge. 'Aren't we past all this?', he muttered to himself, as he decided to skip the whole thing. Blake, like many White Americans, saw direct discussion of racial difference as divisive. When he told Thurston, then his mentor, about his reaction, Thurston challenged him to think again and – at his suggestion – Blake soon went on a couple of week-long IVCF service projects in Black-majority inner-city areas of Virginia. He also began befriending and listening to the stories of African American students and staff. As he began to understand them, so too his awareness grew that whiteness was not neutral: he, as much as Thurston, had a distinct culture and ethnicity which came with its own baggage, bad and good.[66]

The 'White Lounge', which Blake attended the next year, turned out to be a helpful experience with white students from across the region expressing their own perspectives. The writer Robin D'Angelo coined the term 'white fragility'

---

[66] A couple of good books on this from a white perspective are: Daniel Hill, *White Awake: An Honest Look At What It Means To Be White* (IVP: 2017), and: Paula Harris & Doug Schaupp, *Being White: Finding Our Place In a Multiethnic World* (IVP, 2000).

to describe the fact that, because whites are the largest and most culturally dominant group in the United States, they are often able passively to exempt themselves from engaging with the racial tensions consistently and unavoidably encountered by other groups.[67] As Thurston points out, 'It is rarely ever the case that a white person spends six days a week being the minority in their job, neighborhood and social circles, seeing news and entertainment media depicting their people as a negative'.[68] White students, therefore, sometimes react with discomfort and even anger when asked seriously to consider their own position as the beneficiaries of structural racism. They're just not used to it and find it unsettling. In the White Lounge, though, Blake says they discussed all aspects of 'whiteness', including music, art and family customs. He says he went in anticipating imposed shame and guilt, but he instead found a much broader discussion in which he could process his own culture's many good aspects, as well as be honest about its darker edges and impact. And whenever 'white fragility' manifested itself, he says, they were able to discuss and process that together too. They were, he says, 'able to engage in hard conversations but also to offer hope' and show that 'there is possibility for God to redeem "whiteness" in such a way that it is in the likeness of his character'.

Blake says that one key to dealing with racial reconciliation is to understand yourself critically, as an

---

67 Robin DiAngelo, *White Fragility: Why It's So Hard For White People To Talk About Racism* (Beacon Press, 2018).

68 Thurston Benns, 'Black and White [Churches, Forget] Segregation (From 9.25.15 without edits)', on *Benns Blog,* 7 February 2017, https://bennswords. wordpress.com/2017/02/07/black-and-white-churches-forget-segregation-from-9-25-15-without-edits/ (Accessed 28 March 2019).

individual and as part of the various communities from which you hail. Spirituality, as we saw in the physical nature of Jesus' pre- and post-resurrection life, is embedded in contextual specifics. The most *local* place we inhabit is our own body and culture, and therefore, any attempt to ignore what it means to be part of a given national or ethnic group is not only going to be hopelessly detached from reality; it will also be at odds with Jesus' own emphases.[69]

IVCF, like GEU, are able to engage publicly in conversations about justice in places like Urbana, partly because of interpersonal practices on the local level: they are regularly pursuing hard conversations about this and working diligently to ensure that their preaching and discussion is accompanied by a proactive development of student leaders – and staff at every organizational level – from all ethnic and cultural groups.

STARTING NOW

It's easy to look around at one's own culture and feel overwhelmed by The Dump, never-ending racial tensions or whichever else are the big issues where we live. The path of least resistance is simply to avoid these matters. In Guatemala and in the USA, though, the student movements believe that Christians should be participants in the conversations – and action – which shape the culture. The

---

69 Katie Yu, a Korean American staff worker on Blake and Thurston's team who works primarily with Asian students, commented to me that if a missionary goes to another country, they traditionally work overtime to understand their destination's various internal subcultures and identify, and to analyze the assorted people groups and then formulate specific outreach and discipleship · programmes for each one. All IVCF are doing, she said, is applying this to the diverse domestic mission field of the United States college campuses.

place they do this, as a student movement, is primarily in and around the university and among their colleagues.

They don't see this as in tension with proclaiming Jesus, partly because doing so is – as we have seen – following his example, but also because a culturally disengaged faith is an unattractive one. In both Guatemala and the USA, students and staff affirmed that engaging with contemporary issues, especially those pertaining to justice, is a basic Christian value. But several times, from people in both settings, I heard somebody make the offhand remark that, 'This has an apologetic dimension' – meaning that seeing love for Jesus put into concrete action and correlated with all of life made it seem like *more* of a viable option for outsiders (and insiders) otherwise prone to dismiss his relevance. Both evangelism and justice are facets of the single act of partnering with God as he works in the concrete physical locations where we find ourselves.

QUESTIONS FOR REFLECTION OR DISCUSSION:

What are the major issues and problems in your local and national context? How do you think Jesus is of relevance to each of those?

Do you ever feel the pull or tendency to reduce Christian spirituality down to your personal walk with God rather than as something which applies to all of life? What do you think drags you – and other Christians in your context – in that direction?

How could your community imitate GEU's model of focusing on the Scriptures, but doing so in a way which helps participants relate what they read there, not just to their own personal spiritual experience, but also to the city and campus in which they find themselves?

CHAPTER FOUR:
THE PROFESSOR AND THE PERFORMANCE

TALES OF ENGAGING THE UNIVERSITY (SRI LANKA AND GREAT BRITAIN)

Some say he was blown up by his own bomb. Others say he was simply a victim. Whatever the truth, Nimal Balasuriya was a student at the University of Moratuwa on the south-western coast of Sri Lanka, when the homemade device detonated prematurely and cut short his young life. Balasuriya was not the only student to die that year. It was the height of a Marxist-flavoured insurrection in the south of the country that brought the university system to a standstill for two years. Balasuriya was one of many Sinhalese students caught up in the struggle.

Despite his explosive demise, Balasuriya continues to be a presence at the University of Moratuwa, the nation's most prestigious technical institution. A statue of two chained hands, Balasuriya's name inscribed beneath, sits on the edge of campus and forms an enduring reminder of the conflict. For Dr Priyan Dias, Senior Professor in the Civil Engineering Department, it has become such a familiar presence that he barely notices it. Occasionally, though, he glances in its direction and remembers the events of that period and the lives lost. The Vice Chancellor Professor C. Patuwathavithane, for example, was gunned down in his office along with one of his security officers.

Overlapping with the southern insurrection, though stretching over decades rather than years, a civil war raged in the north as Tamil separatist groups fought for the establishment of their own state.[70] Although the theatre of these conflicts was far removed from Priyan's campus, the militants made their presence felt in the rest of the country by, for example, the occasional placing of bombs in public places. The sister of Priyan's research assistant died in such a bus bombing. They were dark times, best left in the past.

Priyan tells me that, as a follower of Jesus, he is constantly asking himself what it means to live out his faith in a country so marked by violence. His position and experience, especially as a successful academic over many decades, lend him immense authority in a culture which tends to revere teachers greatly. Graduating students will often enter a professor's office and kneel in homage as a mark of submission and reverence. Priyan, conscious of Jesus' teaching on the need for leaders to be humble servants and recognizing that teachers are merely fellow students on a university campus, regularly requests that they get up and address him as an equal. Many students are disconcerted when he declines their veneration.

Priyan's commitment to servant leadership, though, extends far beyond such small gestures. During and after the war, he told me, there was great pressure in the country to prioritize loyalty to one's ethnic group over all else. So when

---

70 Sri Lankan Civil War (in the North) was 1983–2009, JVP Insurrection (in the South) was 1987–1989.

he heard that a group of Tamil students had been arrested as potential terrorists after the bus bombing, referred to above, he faced a dilemma. Priyan knew they were mostly peaceful, hardworking individuals and that their arrest had been the product of racial profiling. University authorities took the position that due process should be allowed to happen and declined to get involved in the situation. But Priyan decided to turn up at the police station with another colleague (and fellow FOCUS – the Fellowship of Christian University Students – member) Dr Amal Kumarage, just to stand by the students. It was a risky move as well as a just one; one he feels 'went a long way to building a bridge to the Tamil students on campus'.

Most of the time, though, Priyan's faith is applied in much quieter ways. Writing to a readership of Christian academics and students recently, he told them that one of God's gifts to humanity is our capacity to 'solve sometimes challenging problems that appear intractable … coming up with creative solutions, especially through discourse'.[71] For Priyan, who has only ever worked one year of his life in paid Christian ministry – the twelve months immediately after graduation – the task of research and engineering is as sacred a calling as being a preacher. He, like the North and Central Americans we met in the previous chapter, does not see spirituality as restricted to the non-material realm. Part of what it means to be Christian is to study, teach and innovate in the disciplines – such as civil engineering – which shape our world.

Priyan says he tries to be careful to ensure that he emphasizes the needs of 'the underprivileged and the

---

71 Priyan Dias, 'Thinking Christianly About Engineering', sent to me privately by the author. It has also been included in: *Why Study: Exploring the Face of God in the Academy* (Fellowship of Evangelical Students, 2017).

marginalized ... rather than just helping the rich get richer,[72] as his work is used by governments and corporations to inform their infrastructure projects. It's an approach to academia which is shared by his friend and long-time FOCUS collaborator, Dr Dileni Gunewardena, who is Professor of Economics at the University of Peradeniya, and who has made gender equality a focus of her life's research. Women in Sri Lanka are often marginalized from the workforce and tend to experience disproportionate levels of poverty. Dileni has gained prominence in academia and the Sri Lankan media writing about these topics and proposing solutions, becoming – in the process – a consultant to the World Bank and a member of numerous poverty analysis committees. She even recently spent a semester as Visiting Scholar and Adjunct Faculty at the Economics Department of the American University in Washington DC. Yet she, like Priyan, eschews possible moves abroad in favour of making a permanent home within the Sri Lankan academy.

When I asked Priyan and Dileni about their approach to academia, each of them shared with me a slice of their own biographies. Priyan recalled early memories of his father, a PhD in Agriculture, bringing home academic papers about irrigation and crop science and enthusing him about the tangible benefits of thorough research projects. Dileni remembered a destitute and pungent man who used to sell small, worthless plants outside her church's building in a desperate attempt to raise cash. He became for her a vivid picture of how God's image has become distorted in humanity and our urgent need to work for the restoration

---

72 Dias, 'Thinking Christianly About Engineering.'

of dignity among the marginalized.[73] But amongst all these vivid vignettes, a curious phrase was repeated by both of them – 'the FOCUS ethos'. As I began questioning them each on this concept, I discovered that it held the key to understanding both of their life stories. Making sense of it meant plunging back into the days when the conflicts were just beginning – when Balasuriya was still alive.

THE FOCUS ETHOS

It was supposed to last a year. Vinoth had just received his PhD in nuclear engineering from the University of London and was ready to embark on an illustrious academic career. Numerous opportunities for research positions were potentially available to him across the United States and Western Europe. Before making any final decisions, though, he decided to take a pause and spend twelve months investing in the fledgling student movement back home in Sri Lanka. Many new local campus-based Christian groups had emerged across the country in recent years and Vinoth had been offered a job helping to bring them together into a coherent and sustainable movement.

His years in London had been eye-opening. The Universities and Colleges Christian Fellowship (UCCF), a founder movement of IFES and among the oldest Christian student movements in the world, had long been encouraging its graduates to pursue academic careers. Two of UCCF's leading lights at the time were Sir Norman Anderson, decorated Professor of Oriental Laws at the University of London and renowned expert on Islamic law,

---

73 She also mentioned her Roman Catholic father's efforts to integrate his life and faith.

CAMPUS LIGHTS

and Dr Donald MacKay, Professor of Communication and
Neuroscience at Keele University. Each had made stellar
contributions to their own fields of study and garnered the
respect of their colleagues, all whilst remaining publically
Christian and determined not to divorce their faith from
their studies. In addition to their research interests,
they had published books to help believers (Anderson's
becoming standard UCCF texts on the resurrection and
religious pluralism) and mentored younger academics
(MacKay founding the organization *Christians in Science*
and becoming a 'distinguished thinker in the area of
religion and science'[74]).

Vinoth says that the example of Anderson and MacKay,
among others, caused him to rethink what it meant to grow
a student movement. He began to see that there was a subtle
distinction between 'reaching students' and 'reaching
the university'. It would be all too easy, he realized, to
return to Sri Lanka and develop the equivalent of an
interdenominational church youth group which happened
to target students and meet on campus. But now he saw
the need for something more. The work in Sri Lanka, he
realized, must engage every level of university life.

Stefan Collini, Professor of Intellectual History and
English Literature at Cambridge University, says that
the university is a tricky institution to define, but it
preferably includes 'the ideal of the untrammeled quest for
understanding'.[75] In his book, *What Are Universities For?*,
he writes:

[74] Norman Anderson, *The Evidence for the Resurrection* (IVP, 1959); Norman
Anderson, *Christianity and World Religions: The Challenge of Pluralism* (IVP,
1984); Paul Helm, 'The Contribution of Donald MacKay' in *Evangel* (Winter
1989), pp.11-13.

[75] Stefan Collini, *What Are Universities For?* (Penguin, 2012), p.60.

Major universities are complex organisms, fostering an extraordinary variety of intellectual, social and cultural activity, and the significance and value of much that goes on within them cannot be restricted ... to a single generation .... They have become an important medium – perhaps the single most important institutional medium – for conserving, understanding, extending, and handing on to subsequent generations the intellectual, scientific, and artistic heritage of mankind.[76]

Together with the academic side, which is the focus of Collini's description, many universities also include a web of student-led societies, perhaps a politically-vocal Student Union, a range of non-academic staff including everyone from administrators to janitors, and maybe even religious or pastoral staff, depending on the origins of the university. Universities also include physical locations such as lecture halls, dormitories, cafeterias, clubs, bars, shops, offices and sports fields.[77] To fully engage the university means to be maximally present and involved with the places, people, events and enterprises occurring across the institution. A Christian student movement should, Vinoth became convinced, ideally be a community collectively committed to engagement with university as a whole and not solely to the personal salvation of individual students.

'The FOCUS Ethos',[78] which emerged after Vinoth's return from London, is an ideal pattern for those graduates

---

[76] Collini, *What Are Universities For?*, p.198.

[77] Varying, obviously, from context to context.

[78] 'The FOCUS Ethos' is not an official term – just a popular shorthand among several people with whom I spoke.

of (FOCUS) – the Sri Lankan IFES movement – who decided to pursue an academic career. It involves going abroad to pursue doctoral studies at the highest possible level and then, instead of remaining and making a comfortable life for yourself, returning home and becoming a servant of the Sri Lankan university and also of the student movement. Vinoth, ironically, never pursued this path himself. After one year on staff with FOCUS, he wrote to IFES and asked if they would help fund him for the foreseeable future so that he could fully establish the student movement and also raise up a generation of Sri Lankan graduates, including academics, who thoughtfully applied their faith to their work. There were, when he began on staff in 1980, few – if any – Christian lecturers or professors who integrated faith with life. Ruth Surenthiraraj, the Graduate Staff Worker for FOCUS, tells me that there was a tendency either to 'forcefully introduce' one's faith or – more commonly – simply to maintain an 'elaborate balance between two seemingly disparate worldviews'; one for the workplace and the other for one's 'private' life. Something new was needed. Thoughtful engagement was rare.

Priyan was one of the first to follow the FOCUS Ethos and in 1986 he, like Vinoth, returned from London with a PhD and four years of experience at All Souls, Langham Place, where he became part of a reading group led by IFES Vice President John Stott, which sought to develop Christian responses to popular trends reflected in 'secular' books.[79] He immediately returned to his position at the University of Moratuwa. Within three years, however, a bomb had

---

79 Vinoth had also been part of this group when he lived in London.

killed Balasuriya. Vice Chancellor Patuwathavithane had been assassinated in his office and violence had become part and parcel of campus life in Sri Lanka. The government had taken the decision by then to suspend their entire university system. For two years, professors were still paid and students remained enrolled. But no classes occurred. When I asked Priyan how he filled his time, he recalled to me with a smile that he 'played a bit of cricket' during the pause in academic life.

But Priyan also did something else. Vinoth, Priyan and the FOCUS team took the critical decision that, even though faculty life was on pause, the student movement would not be taking a hiatus. They instead continued to gather students and budding academics for discussion around the Scriptures. Vinoth recalls leading Bible studies from this period, and seeing Christians, Hindus, Muslims, students from the majority Sinhalese ethnic group and members of the radical separatist group, the Tamil Tigers, come together to discuss the issues of the day. Questions he had never heard raised in the vastly different British setting of UCCF – ethnicity, violence and poverty, for example – seemed at the forefront of everyone's mind as they plundered the Bible for ways to answer them. University may have been suspended but the traditional task of academia, which Collini calls 'the untrammeled quest for understanding', was continuing in FOCUS small groups around the country.

When university life formally resumed in 1990, and Priyan laid aside his cricket bat, FOCUS was ready. For the preceding two years they had been developing an acute understanding of how the Bible related to the questions of their context. Christian students and academics were thoroughly prepared to engage in the discussions and debates which would soon emerge in and outside the classrooms in the aftermath of the war. A few months later, Dileni returned from her doctoral studies in Washington DC and – following the FOCUS ethos – joined the faculty of the University of Peradeniya. She reconnected with Priyan and they, together with Vinoth and others, accelerated the work of cultivating new Christian academics. At the most recent meeting of FOCUS' academics' network, there were around ten younger Christian academics along with a number of more experienced ones. Ruth told me that they are now developing a number of further specialized networks around the theme of 'Faith and Work', the first three being for Christians in education, law and engineering. Striking developments in a setting where little, if any, application of faith to work was known less than forty years ago.

EVERYONE EVERYWHERE

Priyan and Dileni are following in an ancient tradition which stretches back to the first century and beyond: they are making the locus of their missional activity the place where they live and work. Through the way they study, teach and wield their varying degrees of influence on campus and beyond, they represent Christ in settings where no church building could ever be constructed. We already saw, in the previous chapter, that true spirituality occurs in concrete physical settings and is expressed through often-painful engagement with all aspects of our world. This was the pattern of Jesus' life, as it is to be of ours.

We cannot follow this pattern unless we choose to embed ourselves in specific local contexts. One day over dinner, Jesus pulled out his iPad and opened Google Maps. Typing in 'Jerusalem', he pointed his finger towards it and said 'you need to be my witness here'.[80] Then, pinching finger and thumb together across the screen, he zoomed the image out to the whole surrounding area. 'Also,' Jesus said, waving his hand over the glowing screen, 'all around here, in Judea and Samaria.' The disciples nodded, knowing the first area well, despite many of them being from the neighbouring region of Galilee. They'd also visited the second and at least had some contacts there.[81] Finally he stretched his digits right out and then brought them together a couple of times until the map showed oceans and vast spreading lands. 'In fact,' Jesus looked around at each of them, huddled around the device as he spoke, 'I'll be wanting you to go right to the edges of this map, to the ends of the earth'. Some of the places seemed blurry, like something was there but couldn't be made out – especially as their eyes ranged further to the east, west and south. Caledonia, Thule and Hispania were visible, Ethiopia, India too – but beyond that it lay unexplored.

Peter pondered Jesus' rather bold plan. It was quite something coming from a man who, for as long as Peter had known him, hadn't even left his own country. Jesus was very much a local homebody. He checked in on his mother regularly, used to work in the building trade as a carpenter – you could see some of the houses he'd worked on around

---

80 This and all other quotations in this paragraph are taken, adapted or praphrased, from Acts 1:8.

81 John 4:39–42.

the Nazareth area – and he was even known to preach sometimes in his local synagogue before that unfortunate incident when the congregation tried to throw him off a cliff for suggesting God might also want to save gentiles such as their Roman occupiers.[82] Peter had heard him speak Greek and Hebrew sometimes, as well as his native Aramaic, but Barbarian and Celtic languages? Here was a local man telling them to go global.

But Peter now knew better than to second-guess Jesus. Events of recent weeks, especially the whole 'check me out, Peter, I'm not dead any more' incident, had increased Jesus' authority in Peter's eyes to the point where his reflex was more towards obedience than renegotiation. He was, then, already processing Jesus' plan when he remembered what had been the topic of conversation right before the iPad came out. He'd instructed them *not* to leave Jerusalem under any circumstances.[83] Now he was telling them to go everywhere. How did the two fit together? Maybe, Peter wondered, it had something to do with his promise that something was going to happen while they remained grounded in Jerusalem. That's right, he'd said not to leave *until* the Holy Spirit had come.

Jesus had been running teaser trailers for the Holy Spirit for three years now. Actually, his cousin John was the first one to raise the topic: he'd said that Jesus would baptize with 'the Holy Spirit and fire'.[84] Some time later, Jesus began to speak occasionally about the Spirit who, he

---

82 Luke 4:14–29.

83 Acts 1:4.

84 Luke 3:16.

told his followers, would live 'with you and ... be in you'.[85] He would be the presence of God with the community of Jesus' followers and, indeed, within its members. Jesus' bodily presence with them was to be temporary, but the Spirit would continue his work among them and remain with them 'for ever'.[86]

But the Spirit wasn't given only for their own comfort, though that is one of his purposes. Almost every time the Spirit is mentioned by Jesus, it occurs in close conjunction with teaching about engagement with the wider world. The Spirit, he says, will be 'speaking through' his followers as they travel with his message and face arrest, will enable them to live for him in inhospitable circumstances, and when Jesus tells them they are the agents to extend and imitate his mission – that 'as the Father sent me, so I send you' – the very next topic of conversation is the Holy Spirit.[87] The Spirit of God is with us, Jesus says, that we might live and speak for – indeed *with* – him in the world God loves.

Peter recalled the stories about the Holy Spirit he'd grown up on. Key leaders throughout his nation's history had been anointed by the Spirit for God's service – Moses, Elijah, Elisha, Samson among others. Jesus, however, didn't ever seem to specify to whom he was sending the Spirit. Was it to his inner circle of twelve, to fewer ... or to more? The answer came a few days later. Around 120 of Jesus' followers were praying together when Peter felt the air unexpectedly rustle his clothes and brush against his

---

85 John 14:17.

86 John 14:16.

87 Matthew 10:20, Mark 13:11, Luke 12:12, John 14:15–19, John 20:21–23.

ears. Looking around he saw that everyone else was being buffeted by the same 'blowing of a violent wind'.[88] Then his eye was caught by a bright, flickering flame hovering above them. As he was still processing this, the fire began to proliferate into numerous similar flames and – as he traced their descent – he observed their complete lack of selectivity: they were resting 'on each of them'.[89] The Spirit had come and he was here to empower *the whole church* and not just a few leaders.

And so, as they ranged ever further from that room, the early followers of Jesus took the presence of God with them. Famous preachers and writers like Peter and John were among them. But also simply ordinary believers going about their everyday business. Research shows that the early church initially spread around the port cities of the Mediterranean.[90] One historian comments that 'the primary bearers of the new faith were rank-and-file believers who travelled for commercial or personal reasons'.[91] The church spread like wildfire because these merchants, and other ordinary folk, believed that God went with them as individuals and as a community.

Peter's conundrum – 'how could the church imitate the local Jesus by becoming a global movement?'[92] – was partly solved by his followers as they travelled,

---

[88] Acts 2:2.

[89] Acts 2:3.

[90] See, for example: Rodney Stark, *Cities of God: The Real Story of How Christianity Became an Urban Movement and Conquered Rome* (HarperOne, 2007).

[91] Stark, *Cities of God*, p.73. See also: Stephen B. Bevans & Roger P. Schroeder, *Constants in Context: A Theology of Mission for Today* (Orbis Books, 2004), pp.74-98.

[92] Not a biblical quote.

embedding themselves in the local contexts where they found themselves. 'As the Father has sent me, I am sending you'[93] came true as they, in the Spirit's power, imitated his willingness to be fully a part of whatever context they found themselves in. Lamin Sanneh, the Ghanaian theologian, has described a key feature of the Christian faith as its 'translatability'.[94] He writes:

> *The New Testament describes Christian Gentiles and others as bonding with Christianity not by tying themselves to the apron strings of Jesus' Jewish origins but by clothing themselves with the authentic vestments of their own culture. Jewish Christian leaders themselves, chiefly Peter and Paul, were the first and most adamant in urging ... such a radical move.*[95]

When Priyan and Dileni chose to live and speak for – and *with* – Jesus on the campuses of Sri Lanka, they were following a pattern which runs throughout the New Testament and all of church history. They believe that the Spirit is with them as they teach, lecture, interact with students, write and research. There is no stone temple, not even the local church building, which is the locus of

---

[93] John 20:21.

[94] Lamin Sanneh, *Disciples of All Nations: Pillars of World Christianity* (Oxford University Press, 2008), p.25.

[95] Sanneh, *Disciples of All Nations*, pp.55–56.

God's activity on earth;[96] he is present wherever we are and 'wherever two or three are gathered in his name.'[97] We, and our community, are the temple of God, the hub of his activity.

Most people featured in this book live in places Jesus described as 'the ends of the earth.'[98] Peter would be amazed to see the way that Jesus' command to be his global witnesses has extended to places which weren't even on his map when he first heard those words. Student movements are a continuation of this pattern: they pick a specific local setting – the university campus – and throw themselves fully into it. They do the things described in the previous

---

[96] In the New Testament after Jesus' ascension, the word 'temple' is used to refer to physical locations such as the Second Temple in Jerusalem, or to pagan temples. But even the Jerusalem temple swiftly fades from significance in Christian life and worship. When 'temple' is used in relation to Christians or the church, it is – Revelation's unique usage aside – usually either used to refer to either individual Christians (e.g. 1 Corinthians 6:19) or to the gathered community of Jesus' followers (e.g. 1 Corinthians 3:16, 2 Corinthians 6:16, Ephesians 2:21). We as individuals, and we as a community, are the place God's manifest presence dwells. Interestingly, no church buildings seem to have been constructed until over two hundred years after the resurrection (the first known one was in Syria, around AD 240, though others cite a location in Jordan from the 290s). None of this is to say that church buildings don't have a useful practical purpose in many settings, just that our understanding and use of them needs to be framed by New Testament teaching on the Spirit and mission. For a good book on the theme of church community as temple, see: Gordon Fee, *Paul, the Spirit and the People of God* (Baker: 1996). For an interesting article on early church buildings, see: Everett Ferguson, 'Why and when did Christians start constructing special buildings for worship?', *Christianity Today*, 12 November 2008, https://www.christianitytoday.com/history/2008/november/why-and-when-did-christians-start-constructing-special.html (Accessed 28 March 2019).

[97] Matthew 18:20.

[98] Literally; Scotland (or Caledonia, to the Romans), located a few hundred miles north of Northampton, the location featured in the second half of this chapter, and Sri Lanka (Serendivi) would have been right at the outer edge of the geographical consciousness of those living in the first century Roman Empire.

two chapters – invitationally proclaiming Jesus and engaging holistically with their context – in the student and university world. Student ministry, like Jesus' own life and work, has an identifiable geographical focus.

NAOMI'S STORY

Naomi was close 'to the ends of the earth' when she opened her mouth to speak. At the very least she was brushing the perimeters of her own comfort. But she didn't remain silent. 'Wonder,' she explained to everyone present, 'is a feeling of amazement and admiration, caused by something beautiful, remarkable, or unfamiliar … When was the last time you *felt* wonder? True wonder. I'm not referring to the wonder you express after eating a really good baguette – "mmm that was wonder-ful." Yes, you might be full, but are you actually full of wonder?'

The room was completely dark as she spoke from the stage, save for a small projected screen. Numerous unseen faces absorbed her every word. Parents, yes. But also her classmates, flatmates, tutors and other curious parties from around the university. Some were friends and others were strangers. They came to witness the final act of Naomi Hollands' three years studying at the University of Northampton, a 12,000-student institution located in the East Midlands of England, which borrows its name from a medieval institution dissolved in the 1200s by King Henry III for – among other things – posing a threat to Oxford and siding with rebellious barons.

The present-day University of Northampton is much less focused on fomenting anti-royalist uprising and is instead best known for its degrees in practical subjects such as business and management, metallurgy, art, education and health. Naomi, as a student of acting and creative practice, had been required – by way of an applied dissertation – to script and present a half-hour piece to the students and staff of the Performing Arts department. She chose to build hers around reflections on her experience and understanding of God. It was a bold move. Not least because it would determine her final grade.

Naomi spent the weeks before performing *W?nder* in a constant state of tension. Everything she tried to write or outline seemed useless. One idea, which combined the use of red balloons and clowning with elements from a well-known sketch about faith, caught her imagination for a while. But the physical logistics of the piece were too great to pull together with her available preparation time. She says she came close to breakdown in a conversation with her tutors just three days before the deadline for submitting her script. It was a Friday and she literally had nothing to give them on the Monday.

Weekends were normally taken up with her part-time job as a theatrical supervisor. But Naomi walked out of the meeting with her tutors and immediately called in to request the day off. She spent her whole Saturday just writing at the desk beside her bedroom window. Whatever came to mind she typed into her laptop. Thousands of words came out. Far from reducing her stress, however, each fresh line simply seemed to increase the tension. She says the immensity of what it all meant – both in terms of speaking to people about God and also as her final coursework project – pushed down increasingly hard on her until, at 10pm, she finally just stopped, turned out her light and stared into the cloudless night outside.

As she slumped in her chair, exhausted from the day's efforts, Naomi's eye was caught by the array of stars in the sky. She began to reflect on how God was bigger than any of her current struggles. Her sense of awe, which also brought her a sense of safety and calm, then gave rise to a simple thought: what if her whole presentation were simply to raise the question of whether God was not the supreme object of wonder we all seek? Other thoughts came crashing in from throughout the previous years – fragments from the Gospel of John, an episode of the Netflix series *Black Mirror*, experiences and conversations she'd had as a student – and she scribbled it all down and gave it shape. By Monday morning she was able to walk into her tutor's office with a combination of confidence in her new direction and mild apprehension about whether it would be supported.

Her tutor, not a Christian, loved the idea. She liked the personal nature of it. But more than that, there was a flow and structure which made her affirm warmly to Naomi that 'this could work'. Approval gained and smiling again, Naomi's next move was to contact Esther Woodall, the local full-time staff member for UCCF, the UK-based IFES movement. Naomi had been a member of the University of Northampton Christian Union, one of over 200 local campus groups supported by UCCF around the country, since she joined the university. Esther Woodall, an English and drama graduate from Royal Holloway University in London, who had moved to support local Christian Unions a few months previously, was delighted to meet and she became Naomi's sounding board as *W?nder* moved from script to reality.

When she finally stepped on stage some days later, Naomi had created a beautifully simple piece of theatre which moved from a dark opening to blending together monologues from various characters – a child full of awe at the world, a student beaten down by the expectations of others, a contemporary reimagining of biblical figures, such as the woman at the well – with music and pre-recorded video segments. It all culminated in a brief personal monologue tying all the characters' experiences to her own:

> Hello, my name is Naomi Hollands, I'm twenty-one years old, and when I was little, I wanted to be a writer. I have 1,141 friends on Facebook, I have 620 followers on Instagram and I get an average of seventy views on my Snapchat stories. I've only ever had one boyfriend but that doesn't mean I don't want one. I cried a lot on my A-Level results day, I already know that the best I can graduate with is a second-class honours degree, which is fine, but it's not a first ... Trying to create this piece of theatre, I've completely changed the idea once and cried twice because it wasn't working out how I had planned, despite saying I don't actually care about the grade. I've never been the prettiest or the most popular, and I have definitely done stuff I'm not proud of. But I am truly satisfied.

She then went on to explain how she had found satisfaction in Jesus' love and acceptance of her, before saying:

> I'm not here to preach a sermon at you, but I can tell you myself that I am truly satisfied. It's not really a feeling I can explain, but the sheer wonder of his love for someone like me blows me away every time, that he loves me and everyone in this room so much he was willing to die on a cross for us, no matter who we are, or what we have or haven't done. And knowing that

THE PROFESSOR AND THE PERFORMANCE

wonder is what truly satisfies me, more than anything in the world ever could. Sure, I'll still want for things like a couple of extra likes on a picture, and I want to be accepted by others – it's human nature. The difference is that I don't feel I need to chase satisfaction, because my soul is truly satisfied.

A few moments later, after a final poetic meditation on the theme of satisfaction, she was receiving a standing ovation. One classmate came to her in tears saying, 'That's what I need – tell me more about it.' Another, who suffered with serious drug issues, came and told her that her performance had made him feel alive like nothing he had ever experienced. More than sixty students came and took copies of John's Gospel, which she had left on a table at the back of the theatre.

One blogger, who arrived at the performance sceptical due to being an 'unreligious person', wrote the following week that 'Hollands performs the whole piece in a confident and believable way, and despite my initial concern, I left thinking about the themes raised'. This, they commented 'is the most wonderful thing we can receive' from theatre.[99]

MISSION AS TEAM

Naomi had been able to take the message of Jesus into the heart of the university. Not through a specifically Christian event or by handing out leaflets. She had done so simply as a natural part of a course assignment. Like Fouad in

---

[99] 'Review of UoN Fringe: Wonder (W?nder) by Lamplight Theatre at The Platform, Northampton' on *A Small Mind at the Theatre*, 29 March 2018, http://asmallmindatthetheatre.blogspot.com/2018/03/review-of-uon-fringe-wonder-wnder-by.html (Accessed 28 March 2019).

his Islamic Studies class, she found that being a Christian student opened doors to speaking publically of her faith. Naomi, of course, was in a context where religious freedom is much more firmly ingrained than in Fouad's Middle Eastern university.[100] But the simple fact of legal liberty to do these things does not automatically lead to them occurring. It took something special.

Naomi's creation and performance of *W?nder* was not, as it appears at first glance, simply a work of individual genius or even just direct divine prompting. It grew, in part, out of the Christian community in which she was embedded. Naomi became involved in the Christian Union during her first year as a student. She was a regular part of the group, lending a hand at various events, but was mostly absorbed by other things; her first two semesters, she told me, were marked by unhealthy friendships and broken trust from fellow students, along with a lingering sense of homesickness and a creeping sense of disillusionment with the entire enterprise of professional theatre.

But, according to Naomi, her second year had been transformational. Involvement in the Christian Union began to shift her perspective on campus life as a whole. British Christian Unions, like all IFES groups around the world, consider the university to be their mission field. Naomi's outlook became increasingly shaped by participation in a community which was always asking questions like, 'how can we serve this campus?' and 'what's the best way to engage our colleagues with the message of Jesus?' She became active in organizing events on campus such as a Christmas Carol Concert which, despite the Christian

---

[100] See Chapter Two (in case you're skipping around this book!).

Union numbering just fifteen active members, managed to attract over sixty guests. Many of Naomi's classmates were among them and had lots of questions for her afterwards.

It wasn't a coincidence that lots of Naomi's friends turned up at the Carol Concert. Christian Unions try to hold in tension two important emphases: the first of these is that living and speaking for Jesus is not a solo enterprise. Christian Unions aim to be the team which implements collective missional projects and that also supports the individual witness of each member. But, as a second accent, Christian Unions also stress the need for each follower of Jesus to be a fully-engaged member of the university. John Stott famously popularized the idea of 'rabbit-hole Christians' who scurry between Christian meetings, minimizing all contact with the wider world.[101] Regular IFES collaborator Rebecca Manley Pippert describes how this works on campus:

A Christian student leaves his Christian roommate in the morning and scurries through the day to class, only to frantically search for a Christian to sit by (an odd way to approach a mission field). Thus he proceeds from class to class. When dinner comes, he sits with the Christians in his dorm at one huge table and thinks, 'What a witness!' From there he goes to his all-Christian Bible study, and he might even catch a prayer meeting where Christians pray for the non-believers on his floor. (But what luck that he was able to live on the only floor with seventeen Christians!) Then at night he scurries back to his Christian roommate. Safe! He

---

[101] Stott says he borrowed this phrase from Major W. Batt. See: John Stott, *Our Guilty Silence* (Eerdmans, 1969), p.62.

made it through his day, and his only contacts with the world were those mad dashes to and from Christian activities.[102]

Pippert's wry description is clearly exaggerated for comic effect. But the danger is real and Christian Unions – like other IFES groups around the world – actively discourage disappearing completely into the community of believers. They may be the only student society on most UK campuses consistently to urge their members to join other societies and make relational connections with outsiders. Involvement in other activities, far from being a threat to the thriving of Christian Unions, is a fulfilment of their own *raison d'être*. It's hard to meaningfully realize Jesus' imperative to bear witness to all lands and people when your world consists mainly of other Christians.[103]

So Naomi, with the encouragement and backing of her Christian Union, had a large circle of friends and was an integrated member of the acting and creative practice student community. Her friends came to the Carol Concert as a natural outcome of the friendship she had with them rather than any particular desire to think about the story of Jesus. Naomi was surprised, therefore, by their intrigue at the basic gospel message communicated by the Concert's speaker. They had so many questions that she proposed a series of three get-togethers – dubbed 'God Chat' – where they would come to her house and talk about their questions. Sixteen of them, all unfamiliar with the Christian faith, came along.

---

102 Rebecca Manley Pippert, *Out of the Saltshaker & Into the World: Evangelism as a Way of Life* (IVP, 1999), pp.113-114.

103 Matthew 28:19–20.

The following year her Christian Union, like most others across the country, ran its annual week of intensive outreach events. 'Mission weeks', as they are known internally, are designed to give curious and sceptical students a focused opportunity to investigate the Christian faith. The main speakers for the week – titled 'Illuminate' – were Joe Winstone, a graduate of another Christian Union, along with future Ichtus (IFES Belgium) staff worker Olivier Le Jeune. Joe and Olivier built their messages around passages from John's Gospel. They used these to address questions such as: 'Life in a Suffering World: Where Do We Even Begin?', 'Life without Filters: Who Am I?' and 'Life of Fresh Starts: How Can I Make the Most of Uni?' Naomi's friends again came along and again reacted with interest. Students who wanted to find out more were invited to sign up for a four- to six-week series of discussions around the Gospel of John called 'Uncover'. Christian students would lead 'Uncover' and, in preparation for doing so, the Christian Union had spent a year of their weekly meetings studying passages from John and applying what they learned to their own lives and to the situation on campus.

Being part of a visible Christian community on campus, then, helped Naomi as she sought publically to live out her faith. It also encouraged her to connect relationally with her classmates despite the breaches of trust she had experienced in her first year. Her friends' reaction to the message of Jesus after the Christmas Carol Concert and mission week grew in her a confidence that those outside the church are actually interested in God if we engage them thoughtfully and creatively. And so, when she came to create *W?nder*, she did so as someone happy to be known as a Christian and confident that anything she said about God would likely be received with interest by her colleagues. She also came armed with a year of reflection on the stories of Jesus, as recorded in John's Gospel and discussed in their weekly Christian Union meetings, which enabled her to weave scriptural themes and narrative fragments creatively back into her work in a way which captivated and challenged an audience of colleagues, tutors and curious onlookers.

CHURCH AND CAMPUS

There is, occasionally, a little discomfort among Christians when they hear of student movements. One pastor articulated his concerns to me quite clearly, shortly after a beautiful evening with his church. There had been five baptisms that night. I knew all the students personally and celebrated as I heard their stories of coming to faith. Each one was welcomed as a member of the local church before friends and family. Though I was a member of another congregation, which meets across town and is affiliated with a different denomination, I also shed tears of joy for the work of God in the lives of each baptismal candidate. I made a mental note to reconnect with the Senior Pastor. We hadn't seen each other in some time and such meetings, designed to strengthen communication and connections between individual churches and university Christian Unions, were a routine part of my then-role as a UCCF Staff Worker.

When we met in his study, a few weeks later, we exchanged pleasantries and caught up on one another's personal lives. I enquired about how the church was going and was delighted to hear good things. As the conversation went on, however, I got a sense that he was waiting for the chance to say something less cordial. Eventually it came. He told me, 'Look, I appreciate your passion, but really we believe in the local church and the only reason your work exists is because local churches aren't doing their job – if they were then you'd be out of business.' It was quite the statement. I suppose I could have taken offence at this but it wasn't the first time I'd heard this perspective. I actually appreciated his directness and sincerity and thanked him for what he shared.

'But,' I insisted, 'we believe in the local church too.' He looked sceptically at me, seemingly pondering how to formulate a polite rebuttal. 'Remember your baptisms last month,' I continued, 'did you notice that three of those students came to faith through the university Christian Union and the other two only found out about you because we encourage all new students to join a local church?' He paused, stared ahead in deep thought for a moment, and then replied, 'I actually hadn't made that connection.' His whole manner rapidly thawed and so did the conversation. We began to speak about the ways his congregation and the Christian Union could partner together for the benefit of the campus and the student community.

There is a myth, ever so pervasive, that church and campus groups ordinarily exist in competition with one another. The truth, however, is that every person profiled in this chapter is an active member of their local church. Priyan and Vinoth are regular preachers at their – and other – local Anglican churches, as well as both having previously served on Theological Commissions for their denomination.[104] Dileni, likewise, is on the worship team,

---

104 Priyan with his diocese's Standing Committee and Theological Commission, and Vinoth with the Theological Commission of the Church of Ceylon (Anglican), along with other committees.

preaching panel and leadership council of her church. Naomi helps run the older youth group at Central Vineyard in Northampton whilst at university and is involved in leading worship at her home church – a Baptist fellowship – when back staying with her parents. Esther Woodall has been involved in youth work at both her previous churches and currently runs a girls' discipleship group at the non-denominational church where she is a member.

IFES groups, in fact, customarily work hard to ensure that every member is aware of local churches and is encouraged to commit to one for the duration of their time as a student. New believers will also invariably end up integrated into a local church. Each person within UCCF and FOCUS, from undergraduates to academics and board members, through to staff and senior management, are usually active members of a nearby congregation. This runs right through to the national leadership of both movements: UCCF Director Richard Cunningham, for example, is an ordained Church of England minister, while FOCUS General Secretary Yohan Abeynaike is on the preaching team at The Church of St Francis of Assisi in Mount Lavinia.

Far from Christian Unions (and other IFES groups) existing 'because local churches aren't doing their job', the reality is the polar opposite – these groups are, in fact, incredible examples of the local church fulfilling its calling by encouraging its members to focus their efforts on a very specific and strategic mission field within their locale or parish: the university or college campus. Unlike much of their other work, however, churches which back IFES encourage students and academics to engage their context in partnership with followers of Jesus who are members of other congregations. Thus the campus group becomes a mission team formed from among the members of numerous local churches. It is a pooling of resources, most especially human ones, for the mission of God in a single unique setting.

For most Christians, unless they end up joining the student movement's staff after graduation or – like Priyan and Dileni – pursuing a career in academia, involvement in campus ministry will be a temporary experience. They'll join the mission team on campus for the duration of their student years and then move on to the workplace and, beyond perhaps financially supporting or praying for the student movement, the campus will rapidly fade into their rear-view mirror. The opportunities to produce a piece of work like *Wo?nder*, present the case for the New Testament to an Islamic Studies class or erect a conversation-starting Christmas tree in the heart of an overwhelmingly Muslim faculty are therefore fleeting and easily missed. A focused team of students, backed by local churches and supported by staff members, can help them maximize their efforts while they're still part of the campus context.

CONTEXTUAL COMMUNITIES

Student movements, then, are not simply missional Christian groups which happen to focus on a particular demographic. They embed themselves in a context, the university (or college or polytechnic), and become full participants who seek the good of that place and those who inhabit and frequent it. It's notable that almost everything described in *Campus Lights* up until this point happened *on* – or as close as legally possible *to* – a campus. Those few examples which did not were special events (like the

Urbana convention in the US, or the Mission Labs in Indonesia) designed, in part, better to prepare students to engage the campus.

In this they continue the mission of Jesus by making specific geographical locations – Jerusalem, Judea, Samaria and the ends of the earth; Sri Lanka, Great Britain, the University of Moratuwa, the University of Peradeniya and the University of Northampton – the places they go in the Spirit's power to live and speak for and with him.

QUESTIONS FOR REFLECTION OR DISCUSSION:

Have you ever considered the difference between reaching students and engaging the university? If you had to list the particulars of each one, how would you do so? Use the chart below:

Reaching Students	Engaging the University

With what areas – geographical, cultural, social or academic – of university life is your Christian community currently unengaged? Maybe places like dorms or clubs, or particular groups of people or something/somewhere else? Make some notes, and perhaps sketch some ideas of how to take action in concert with other followers of Jesus:

If you could commit to praying for one area or aspect of the university (or tertiary educational) world, which one would you choose? Pick groups, people, places or cultural aspects … or anything else that comes to mind. If you're stuck, why not take a prayer walk around campus for inspiration?

CHAPTER FIVE:
BUSINESSMEN AND EMIGRANTS
TALES OF PREPARING GRADUATES
(KENYA AND ROMANIA)

His colleagues' voices blend together in a single polyphonic stream. Their thanksgiving and requests, directed toward their Creator, are uttered with piercing urgency and conviction. Every so often, someone breaks up the intercession by sharing a snippet from the Scriptures or a story of something God has been doing in their life. John Ng'ang'a, who established this little group a few years previously, sits to the side and joins in the prayers. But he doesn't take a lead. As a senior manager in the company, he doesn't want people to participate simply as a means of career advancement. So he has long since handed the group's oversight to his juniors. Now he simply joins in like anyone else.[105]

John wasn't even sure he would start something like this again. Shell, his employer, had headhunted him from the Development Bank of Kenya a few years previously; they were to be his second employer. While at the bank,

---

[105] In addition to my interview with John, this section also leans on John's published works, a list of which can be found at johnnganga.org. John's own autobiographical sketch of life as a Christian businessman is found in the second chapter of: John N. N. Ng'ang'a, *Christian Professionals: Leading in the Marketplace* (Taruma, Consultants, 2012).

he'd started a lunchtime Christian fellowship, as much for himself as anyone else. During his first few weeks in the working world, fresh from graduating in business from the University of Nairobi, he was struck by the unfamiliarity of his new situation. He had, while still a student, conceived of himself as becoming a 'missionary banker'; someone whose work would benefit the poor – whether through direct interventions, like microloans, or via nudging larger corporations towards fairer practices – and whose professional connections would open opportunities to talk about Jesus with those who might not otherwise take him seriously. So he identified and gathered staff already following Jesus and invited them to pray together for one another and also for their colleagues in the bank.

John says that, even many decades later, he still meets people who tell him that they first opened their lives to God through this small band of praying bank employees. When he moved to Shell, however, he found himself in an even less familiar situation. Shell, as a multinational corporation, was – even at the local level – quite a different beast than the Development Bank, and John, now in a more senior management position, found himself treading more carefully than before. He was a foreigner in an international company and his existing instincts may not serve him well here. He says that he felt the best thing to do at this point was to perform his job well and with integrity, treat his subordinates with kindness and respect, and be sure not to hide his own Christian commitment. Anything more formal would have to wait.

One of John's practices was to develop relationships beyond the professional. He would make a point of inviting clients for coffee at his own expense and on his personal time, just to get to know them. He says that many Europeans, visiting Africa for the first time, would arrive with virtually no first-hand knowledge of the Christian faith. It was very natural for religion and spirituality, so unavoidable in the Kenyan context, to land on the conversational agenda. John says that Europeans in Africa became a kind of accidental 'mission field' for him. When John told me this, I couldn't help but think of a question, grounded in ignorance of global religious demographics, which I often heard people ask when I was growing up in Britain: 'But what about all the people in Africa who haven't heard about Jesus?' John would have laughed at this concern, as he was asking himself almost the exact opposite question: 'What about all these people from Europe who know nothing of Christ?'[106]

Eventually, as he found conversations emerging more frequently and some colleagues beginning to call on him as a source of wisdom and direction, he decided it was time to approach the Human Resources department and ask them if a room might be made available for a weekly non-denominational Christian prayer meeting. They readily agreed, and so began a group which continued to meet even after John retired twenty-five years later. Over the years, many came to follow Jesus through these gatherings, which often also included a short Bible talk from one of their Christian colleagues in the company. John himself went on to assume a series of postings that had a wider geographical reach – Uganda, Ethiopia and Tanzania – and

---

106 The answer to the question 'what about people who haven't heard?' is, of course, 'you tell them!' However, it's always easier to keep the discussion on a theoretical level which exempts us from personal action. If, however, you do want a more detailed theoretical discussion of the issue, take a look at: Dennis L. Okholm & Timothy R. Phillips (eds.), *Four Views on Salvation in a Pluralistic World* (Zondervan, 1996).

in each location he initiated a workplace fellowship which eventually ended up being led by others.

When I asked John what led him to live as a 'missionary banker' and 'missionary businessman', his answer was instantaneous: he was ready to live and speak for Jesus in the workplace because he'd done so on campus. He was a missionary businessman, he told me, because he had first been a missionary student. His words reminded me of something I'd once heard from Samuel Escobar, the Peruvian theologian and long-time IFES President. Escobar said that students who 'see their own campus as a mission field, [are] better prepared to see also the entire world as a mission field ... faithful testimony for Christ in the hostile atmosphere of secularized campuses prepared these students to be more sensitive missionaries' wherever else they found themselves.[107] Graduate life, according to both Escobar and Ng'ang'a, is an extension of student life and our values and praxis before graduation spill over, albeit adapted and evolved, into each new setting we enter.

THE SYSTEM

Living and speaking for Jesus in the working world is not straightforward. Not only do we face the challenge of our own characters, but we often also find ourselves coming up against systems and conventions bigger than ourselves.

---

107 From Samuel Escobar's address for the IFES World Assembly in Seoul, South Korea, July 1999, entitled 'A New Time for Mission'. He makes this statement after listing a series of IFES graduates having an impact in diverse settings, including the Middle East, Brazil and the Philippines. An excellent accessible introduction to Escobar, available in multiple languages, is his book: Samuel Escobar, *A Time for Mission: The Challenge for Global Christianity* (Langham Global Library, 2013).

An empty building, tucked away on a backstreet not far from my home, has come to epitomize this challenge for many in our city. It used to house the Colectiv nightclub. The building's now-blackened walls are sealed off from public view. Outside are flowers, candles and photos of the twenty-six young people who died during the few minutes it took the flames to rip through the club. A further thirty-eight passed away later in hospital, and almost 150 suffered varying injuries. Metal band 'Goodbye to Gravity', whose five members were all among the victims, had been using pyrotechnics in their show when a spark ignited the foam wall insulations and poisonous fumes filled the room, rendering many unconscious; they were left to burn while others fled.

It has been over three years since the Colectiv nightclub fire and the location remains a shrine visited by people each day. The display outside the Colectiv is not simply a memorial to the dead: the fire had a profound impact on the outlook of young Romanians because, in the tragedy's aftermath, it was alleged that the event was a direct result of corrupt practices on the part of club management and local government. Basic fire regulations had seemingly been wilfully overlooked, a venue with a capacity of eighty had been filled with several hundred people and the district mayor was accused of having 'granted a permit for the club despite it not being authorised by firefighters'.[108] The blaze became emblematic of a culture of corruption seen by many as endemic to Romanian politics and commerce.

108 Staff and Agencies, 'Romanian prosecutors arrest local mayor over Bucharest nightclub fire', *The Guardian*, 7 November 2015, https://www.theguardian.com/world/2015/nov/07/romanian-prosecutors-arrest-local-mayor-over-bucharest-nightclub-fire (Accessed 28 March 2019).

Tens of thousands took to the streets, and within a few days the prime minister, the district mayor and the minister of internal affairs had all resigned.

Despite the outcry, however, corruption didn't suddenly diminish in Romania. How could it? Something so ingrained cannot be shaken within a week. The problem here is not the ethics of individual workers but the system within which they have to operate. Graduates entering the workplace quickly encounter a structure where backhanders and shortcuts are frequently the path to immediate success, and sometimes the only way to survive the corruption seems to be to become part of it. Adrian Lauran, one of the pioneers of the Romanian Christian student movement, Organizaţia Studenţilor Creştini Evanghelici din Romania (OSCER), has spent most of his adult life building communities of people who live according to the values of Jesus rather than the culture.

Adrian grew up under the communist dictatorship of Nicolae Ceauşescu. It was a period when you could, at best, be openly Christian in the church building and nowhere else. Even then it was understood that agents in the congregation would, the very next morning, file a police report on the service's contents. When a violent revolution (or coup, depending who you ask) led to Ceauşescu's execution in 1989, new freedoms began to emerge: four previously-underground Christian student groups went public in various cities and a fifth was soon established by around a dozen final-year students in Craiova. When Adrian enrolled at the University of Craiova, just over a year later, they handed the leadership of the group over to him and he began the task of building up an interdenominational student group.

Beginnings were rocky. Local churches, pinned back in their buildings for decades, struggled to apprehend the idea of Christian mission occurring in the heart of a secular institution like the university. Adrian, however, persevered and – under the mentorship of Gelu Paul, a founder of the student group in the western city of Timişoara and a recent graduate of Gordon-Conwell Theological Seminary in the United States – made the focus of his energies a small group of Christian undergraduates. His hope was that as they, like John Ng'ang'a, would learn a new approach to mission on campus and, on graduation, benefit the various churches and workplaces where they were members by bringing a fresh approach to mission. OSCER had, during this period, connected with IFES and Adrian had seen the way that IFES graduates in many European nations did something similar.

Adrian was soon to discover, however, that few churches in the city perceived the need for a different kind of missional focus. They preferred the maintenance of internal programmes. Whenever a non-Christian student turned up on a Sunday – often at the invitation of someone from Adrian's group – with long hair or smelling of smoke, breaking two of the church's cherished taboos, they were made to feel anything but welcome. Many within the student group, which by this time had mushroomed to a weekly attendance of over one hundred people, were pressuring Adrian to start a church which reflected their missional values. Adrian, however, resisted, as he believed firmly in the value of inter-church witness at the heart of the university. So, with delicate diplomatic footwork, he began – separate from the student group – to invest time in a handful of graduate couples, along with a few students, who could eventually form the backbone of a new church.

Eleven years after Adrian began as a student in Craiova, Pro Deo Church launched in the city. It actively supports the local student group but also encourages it to work with a range of churches. Two of Adrian's mentees went on to help plant new churches in the cities of Bucharest and Piteşti. He also acted as consultant, and later associate pastor, to a new church plant in his hometown of Haţeg. In total there are four flourishing churches and at least two local student groups which have emerged in Romania as a result of Adrian's initiative or advice. He is the very definition of a change agent and precisely the kind of person every student movement needs.

These days, however, Adrian is a displaced change agent. He still invests in Romania – when we spoke, he told me that he mentors, from a distance, up to twenty young Romanian leaders – but he now makes his home in Portland, Oregon, where he is planting a church among the second and third generation of Romanian diaspora. Adrian tells me that the move to the USA was a surprising call of God. He says that, while he didn't leave *purely* from disillusionment with the Romanian system, he believes it is one of the instruments God used in his call.[109]

An experience which encapsulates the worst of Romanian culture for Adrian came in the years immediately before he left. A close friend, Florin, had decided to expand his recycling business into something larger.[110] He'd obtained

---

[109] Life is messy, isn't it? And God integrates the mess into his plans for us, meaning that an odd and almost-paradoxical statement like 'God used disillusionment to call me' makes Biblical sense, though one has to be cautious not to use disillusionment as pretext for choosing the easy path. See Romans 8:28. Lindsay Brown, after reading this section, recommended to me the book: George Verwer, *Messiology* (Moody Publishing, 2016).

[110] Not his real name, distinguishing details obscured.

a grant from an international body and hired several new staff. One of his aims was to dramatically improve the environmental impact of the industrial town where he had grown up. Adrian been instrumental in Florin beginning to follow Jesus while a student and, since Florin came from a family with few Christians, he – along with others in OSCER – had become Florin's model of social, spiritual and intellectual life, not to mention of integral leadership and good management. It was through Adrian and OSCER that Florin had gained the vision to return to his hometown and attempt to be of benefit to it.

The project, which began well, slowly fell apart when the local agency responsible for distributing Florin's €800,000 grant began to drag their heels. Florin says it became clear that, despite being locals with a goal of bettering their community, they were outsiders to the political and relational groups who controlled the city. Some people began asking for a cut of the money – bribes simply for doing their job – and when Florin refused, it slowly became clear that they would not give them a penny; they intended to saddle Florin with all the debts and liabilities. Some friends kindly stepped forward and helped Florin out of his most immediate financial difficulties, but the project folded and, within six months, he too was living abroad. He says that disillusionment played a relatively small part in his move – he was simply at a career dead end in Romania and an opportunity, along with a sense of God's prompting, combined to move him across the Atlantic to Canada. But even today he is still paying off the project's debts.

Adrian is well capable of suffering a setback. Anyone who grows up under a communist regime learns to handle adversity with aplomb.[111] The challenge he and Florin faced was more profound than simple personal disappointment: they felt that their faces had been smashed against the same hard wall of corruption which later facilitated the Colectiv fire. Individual integrity and personal passion for sharing Jesus marked their ministry and business lives, of course, but this – while essential for any follower of Jesus – seemed insufficient for getting past the wall. Adrian says that if the system was different then it is unlikely he would have ever left. Florin, likewise, could easily see himself still running his environmental development project. Perhaps he would even have expanded it to other locations.

POWER AND LOVE

Confrontation with the system is an age-old theme. Twenty minutes' walk from the Colectiv nightclub, passing through Bucharest's historic Jewish neighbourhood en route, lies a church building whose early worshippers were refugees fleeing a genocide in their homeland. Holy Archangels Church, built for the city's centuries-old Armenian community in 1915, opened its doors just a few months after the Armenian Holocaust had begun.[112] This horrendous event, one of several such mass killings undertaken by the Ottoman Empire between 1914 and 1923,[113] saw around 1.5 million Armenians slaughtered and hundreds of thousands

---

[111] Aside from the Apparatchiks, the Party officials, of course, who experienced little adversity until purged by their paranoid leader.

[112] Most people refer to it as 'the Armenian church', though it is also called *'Biserica Sfinţii Arhangheli Mihail şi Gavriil', meaning 'The Church of the Holy Archangels Michael and Gabriel'.*

[113] Others include the Greek (1914–1922) and Assyrian (1915–1923) genocides, which also saw hundreds of thousands ethnically cleansed by the Ottomans.

more fleeing. Romania was the first country to offer them asylum.[114]

The first time I visited Holy Archangels was on a chilly spring morning; I was just looking for a quiet place to sit and reflect between meetings downtown. I wandered over, pulled open its heavy wooden doors and stepped inside. I was confronted within by numerous rows of empty varnished wooden pews, surrounded by mostly plain yellow walls and smattered by occasional statues or pictures. Moving further inside, I sat down and – as I rested into the stillness – I found my eyes drawn towards a painting on the curved ceiling ahead of me. It depicted the Trinity: the Father represented as a wise old man with a grey beard, the Spirit as a blue dove emanating golden flames from his outstretched wings and the Son as a bearded, younger man in a robe, with an enormous wooden cross – as tall as him or the Father – propped up under his arm. It struck me, as I contemplated this image, what a striking vision it painted of God: here was a picture of the divine, hovering above me in a place of quietness and meditation, and right in the midst of it was a massive torture instrument.

I thought back to those early Armenian worshippers, many of them refugees and possibly the only members of their families to escape the genocide, and wondered what it must have been like for them to see this hanging above them as they sang and prayed each Sunday. They would be met with an image of a God not distant from their suffering but involved. Pain and brutal oppression by a hostile political system, the picture communicates, has been brought into the life of God himself. The Christian faith, for them,

---

114 Or so people here say; I haven't located a source on this.

was not to be a place to which they fled from their most heartbreaking experiences, but one in which that darkness can be interpreted and healed at the feet of the crucified God. Neither, for me, was Holy Archangels to be a place of escape: it reminded me that the Christian faith, if it is to remain true to its foundations, must not treat pain and struggle as mere side issues.

The next week I was giving a talk entitled 'Where is God in a World of Suffering?' at an OSCER group in a nearby city. I used the Colectiv fire as my starting point. 'If we drew a map of Romania,' I asked, 'where might we sketch in Jesus?' In smoky political meetings, making deals and winking at bribes? Sitting at home crying as he watched events on television? Huddled in a café with friends, helplessly discussing what was happening? Or would we place him in the club as the fire raged – torched alive by a broken system? 'Because,' I noted, 'that is precisely where the New Testament locates him.' This, of course, is comforting: a God who has suffered with us (and for us) is tremendously attractive. But it is also profoundly unsettling.

Jesus, unlike the Colectiv fire victims, wasn't in the wrong place at the wrong time. He chose that path. The scene in Gethsemane, where Jesus is 'overwhelmed with sorrow to the point of death',[115] derives its power partly from Jesus' clear knowledge of what was to occur just a few hours later. His veins seem to be literally bursting with the stress of the coming crucifixion, causing his sweat to appear 'like drops of blood falling to the ground'.[116] He could easily have escaped all this stress. We have a story

---

115 Matthew 26:38.

116 Luke 22:44.

elsewhere in the New Testament of him strolling away from a homicidal mob with the relaxed air of a man brushing dust off his sleeve.[117] But he was also unwavering in his insistence towards his disciples that he would soon sacrifice himself. It was terrifying, but he persevered.

For his followers the very idea was almost impossible to process. When Judas arrives with a detachment of Roman soldiers, some of them even reach for their weapons.[118] They've seen Jesus perform incredible miracles. After one such display of power – the feeding of the five thousand – the people attempted to 'make him king by force'.[119] 'This man,' they may have reasoned, 'is exactly who we need in a confrontation with Rome'. Perhaps his disciples also briefly perceived the moment of Jesus' arrest as the dawn of their nation's liberation from Caesar's system. Those hopes, at least as they held them, were swiftly dashed. He was, as his disciples intuited, well capable of crushing anyone. Yet he told Peter to 'Put your sword back in its place ... Do you think I cannot call on my Father, and he will at once put at my disposal more than twelve legions of angels?'.[120] In hindsight we know that, yes, Jesus was going to defeat the system; firstly through his resurrection and later through his return. But right now his confrontation with the broken and corrupt system of the world involves him being murdered and tortured by it.

Jesus' death was power used for the purposes of love. He could have run or fought, but he remained and died. The

---

117 Luke 4:29–30.

118 John 18:2–12.

119 John 6:15.

120 Matthew 26:52–53, Peter is identified as the man with the sword in the parallel account of John 18:10-11.

cross, of course, soon came to be understood as something he did *on behalf* of humanity. This had been a theme in Jesus' life since his mother was told, prior to his conception, that 'he will save his people from their sins',[121] had continued when his cousin John identified him as 'the Lamb of God, who takes away the sin of the world'[122] and was woven throughout Jesus' own teaching, such as his insistence that he came 'to give his life as a ransom for many'.[123] Jesus, at the cross, was broken as he embraced the world and – in the process – saved us.

Alongside this understanding of the cross runs another: namely, that Jesus' death was not only achieving something *for* us, but was also modelling *how we should live.*[124] 'Whoever wants to be my disciple,' he told his closest followers, 'must deny themselves and take up their cross daily and follow me'.[125] There's a curious tension in this phrase between the words 'cross', referring to a tool intended to terminate life, and its attached adverb, 'daily', which implies something ongoing. Jesus was urging a willingness to imitate his own demise by embracing a broken and poisonous world. But he was also suggesting that this may not lead to instant bodily death but, instead, be followed by yet another day of waking afresh to do it all again. He is urging, in the famous words of Eugene Peterson, 'a long obedience in the same direction'.[126]

---

121 Matthew 1:21.

122 John 1:29.

123 Mark 10:45.

124 Jesus also used a foot-washing ritual, a few hours before his arrest, to spell out for his friends that they were to imitate his willingness to serve each other in humiliating and uncomfortable ways. See: John 13:1–15.

125 Luke 9:23.

126 Eugene Peterson, *A Long Obedience in the Same Direction: Discipleship in an Instant Society* (IVP, 2000).

We are asked to take the cross into our lives as the Trinity have taken it into theirs. To imitate the crucified king by wielding whatever power and influence we may have in the service of love.

Graduates are not exempt from this call. Faced with disconcerting and often unfriendly structures – whether economic, political or cultural – we need followers of Jesus who neither take on the values of the system nor flee from engaging with it. Running or capitulating may seem like the two simplest paths to avoiding pain, but Jesus' call is not towards the easy or the painless. It's towards the costly and the uncomfortable. When things turned nasty for Adrian and Florin, this was *not* God's plan falling apart any more than it was for Jesus at Gethsemane. It was, instead, the normal-yet-uncomfortable path of discipleship as cross-bearing.

ORGANIC MENTORSHIP

When Florin and I discussed his collapsed project, I asked him how he would assess his own part in it: would he say that he'd acted with integrity? Florin replied that he felt that his own actions, and those of his team, had been honest and straightforward. They'd taken up their crosses and made the costly choice to pay no bribes and to tell no lies. They had nothing of which to feel ashamed. But he also told me that it had been a learning experience. In hindsight, he wishes he had made different decisions. By far his biggest mistake, he told me, was not seeking out mentorship from more experienced Christian businesspeople. They could have offered guidance on how to navigate the system successfully, without sacrificing ethical principles. It may have been possible to imitate Jesus' sacrificial posture without their business experiencing such a sudden demise.

When I asked Florin why he didn't do this, he told me that he had two possible answers: some days he tells himself that it was pride and overconfidence, other times he thinks it was simply naïvety – his previous smooth sailing in business led him to believe that a bigger project would only be more of the same, albeit with increased logistical complexity. He didn't anticipate how his larger budget would bring him into the crosshairs of certain interest groups. Florin listed a number of Christian businessmen, either local to him or OSCER graduates from other cities, who he knows personally and who, he was sure, would have been open to him approaching for advice.

Such connections between students and graduates tend to exist naturally within student movements. Graduates often provide the volunteer and paid staff, board members and speakers for local groups, not to mention – as we shall see in Chapter Seven – much of the funding. As a movement grows older, there also tend to be a good number of local church leaders and members whose critical *formación* in mission came through involvement on campus. Because of IFES groups' typically highly-relational ethos, connections form and mentorship opportunities emerge naturally.

Laurenţiu Guşu and Lucian Bălănescu are a great example of this. Their 'meet cute' came during Lucian's first year at university when he snuck into the back of an OSCER meeting in Bucharest. Lucian was, at this point, disillusioned by a series of bad experiences with the church: lies, manipulation, hypocrisy – much of it pointed in his direction – along with a pervasive sense that there was no place in Christianity for people who think and ask questions.

He felt he was on the very fringes of faith. A friend from high school though, suggested that he should at least take a look at OSCER. As he sat listening to an apologetics talk by Laurenţiu, carefully and intelligently unfolding the case for trusting Jesus, Lucian felt like he'd glimpsed something different.

Laurenţiu, at this point, had already been in OSCER for over a decade.[127] He'd joined the movement, in fact, many years before its legal foundation. It was four days after the Romanian Revolution had begun, and five days before dictator Nicolae Ceauşescu was to be executed on national television, that Laurenţiu first found himself – at the behest of a friend – in a Christian student meeting. They were, at this point, a clandestine group meeting underground for fear of academic expulsion or even jail. A few weeks later, however, the communist regime had fallen and the students went public with their movement. They began plastering the faculties with posters advertising a weekly Christian gathering in the heart of the university.

The following years in the movement, Laurenţiu says, shaped him to think of following Jesus as something you put into action wherever you are. When he graduated, he could no longer be satisfied with what seemed to be the basic requirements of a churchgoer in many parts: sitting on the pew every Sunday and trying not to do anything terribly scandalous for the rest of the week. He instead sought spaces to serve in the church and strove hard to connect his

---

127 Or, at least, in OSCER's predecessors: OSCER was constituted from various local groups in 1998. The group in Bucharest was independent (as were all others) when Laurenţiu first joined in 1989. Networking with other future OSCER groups and with IFES grew throughout the 1990s. OSCEB, the current OSCER group in Bucharest, is the offspring of this early underground group.

faith to his work in increasingly senior positions within a series of large companies, and to maintain a reading regime which enabled him to speak intelligently and relevantly to the student world when invited to speak at OSCER events. This last emphasis enabled him to appeal to Lucian when he slipped into the back of a student meeting for the first time.

After Laurențiu's talk, Lucian approached him to express appreciation. As the conversation unfolded, a friendship began. Both men say that there was never a moment when they thought or said, 'let's start a mentoring relationship'. Laurențiu simply began to invite Lucian into his life and home. They spent hours talking together. Laurențiu helped Lucian begin reading books which could help him integrate reason, culture and faith. As Lucian became a member of the leadership team of OSCER's Bucharest group, and then later worked as Chief Operating Officer of 648 Group – an app-focused IT company whose clients included Samsung, Dell and Netflix – he continued to look to Laurențiu as a role model of how workplace faith, right down to the kindly and just treatment of employees, plays out in practice. He learned from Laurențiu the Jesus-like art of wielding power and influence for the purposes of love.

Over his time with 648 Group, Lucian continued to support and encourage OSCER and became increasingly called upon as a speaker at their events, both locally and nationally. His early talks were closer to an imitation of Laurențiu's style, but soon he developed an approach all his own. Not long ago he transitioned from the business world to dividing his time between serving on his church pastoral team and investing in students and young professionals through his role as Director of New Projects for Chrysolis Romania. Even as I write this, he has just returned from giving the Christmas message at the Craiova OSCER group once led by Adrian Lauran, who we met earlier in this chapter. Lucian's experience and integrity in business provides an added element of credibility to his message as he addresses audiences looking for a way to live within the complexities of the Romanian system. Even critics call him 'the voice of evangelical millennials',[128] and it's a responsibility he takes seriously.

Lucian says that, if it were not for Laurențiu, he's not sure where he would be today. Perhaps outside the faith? That doesn't quite fit with Lucian's theology. But he does question whether he would have learned to navigate the working world with integrity, let alone to become someone balanced and confident enough in his own faith to communicate it to others wrestling with questions and doubt. He says he would almost certainly have ended up joining Adrian and Florin, not to mention his emigrant parents, across the Atlantic in North America. Another change agent would have been lost. But Laurențiu had become a mentor and model as Lucian learned to carry his cross daily, first in the Christian student movement, then in the business world and now in church-based and other ministry.

FROM INCIDENTAL TO INTENTIONAL

Laurențiu was a surprise inclusion in this book. He is a personal acquaintance of almost twenty years and Lucian is one of my closest friends and colleagues. I was hesitant to begin profiling the characters who populate my life. But

---

128 Paul Dan, 'Criza tineretului evanghelic si fenomenul Balanescu', *Ioan8*, 19 December 2018, https://ioan8.wordpress.com/2018 (Accessed 28 March 2019).

I ended up contacting him at the suggestion of another Bucharest-based friend, Susan Stone, who is developing a national graduate network in association with both OSCER and also IFES Europe's Graduate Impact project.[129] Susan and I had met for coffee to discuss her perspective on graduate-student integration and she told me about how she shared Florin's conviction that mentorship is a vital component in helping Romanian Christian graduates navigate the business world with integrity and become change agents. She cited Laurențiu and Lucian's relationship as something she would like to see repeated across the nation.

Susan and I had both read the United Nations' statistic that more people had left Romania than any other country aside from Syria between 2007 and 2015.[130] It seems, to anyone who has travelled widely, an odd statistic: Romania is one of the safest countries in the world, the fastest growing economy in Europe and is a nation packed with beautiful mountain ranges, a gorgeous coastline and innumerable ancient castles and churches. It doesn't appear to be a prime candidate for the 'most escaped country' award. Yet Romania is also part of Europe and linked with the rest of the world via the Internet. Romanians increasingly look nearby, especially to places like Germany and the United Kingdom, and perceive that these are locations where you can forge a life for yourself without battling the entire national infrastructure. Many, of course, leave because of financial motivations. But others, like Adrian and Florin,

---

[129] Visit their website: https://www.graduateimpact.org/.

[130] Anca Alexe '3.4 million Romanians left the country in the last 10 years; second highest emigration growth rate after Syria', *Business Review*, 26 February 2018, http://business-review.eu/ (Accessed 28 March 2019).

depart because they've been beaten down by the Romanian system one too many times.[131]

Susan explained that her network would include, among many other things, an intentional pairing of experienced Christian mentors with newly-graduating students entering the workplace for the first time. She wants older medics to invest in younger doctors, seasoned marketers to connect with young PR trainees and emerging academics to come under the wing of long-time professors. 'We often,' she told me, 'ask rather general questions about what it means to follow Jesus: "how can I speak with others about Jesus?", "how can I have integrity?" and "why does work matter?"' These questions area good starting point, she affirmed, but we also need to move to even more concrete ones, like: 'how do I navigate the ethical quandaries of end-of-life medical care?', 'how can honesty and success coexist in the life of a marketer?', or – Susan's favourite – 'what is God's vision for this generation of Romanian engineers?'

Graduates who are to not only remain, and also to do so with impact, will – she believes – be those who are sketching in the detail of what it means to follow Jesus in the specific workplace contexts in which they spend most of their daylight hours. They need to gain a vision for their setting and grasp in realistic terms what it means to be a 'missionary worker', carrying the cross where they are placed. The optimal guides for this are those who have already been there and can use their experience to

---

131 I'm not in the least anti-immigration/emigration, nor unsympathetic to those who leave, which would be an ironic position for me to adopt, as an immigrant married to another immigrant. If systemic problems are a dragon, then the way to respond is not to lock Romanians in the dungeon with it. It is instead to give them the weapons and training to battle the beast for themselves.

help others. What Susan is attempting is simply a more systematized version of what occurred organically when experienced manager and sometime preacher Laurenţiu – when he wasn't doing paid work – began inviting Lucian into his life.

In Kenya they are already fulfilling something similar to the mentoring component of Susan's vision. The student movement there, known as Fellowship of Christian Unions (FOCUS), is twice as old as OSCER and encompasses over 45,000 students in 152 institutions.[132] Graduate mentoring relationships have, as in Romania, long occurred in and around the student movement; folks like John Ng'ang'a and influential Bishop David Oginde have remained connected to the movement and – through student contacts made when they speak at national conferences or local groups – have very naturally ended up mentoring younger believers. George Ogalo, the National Director of FOCUS, told me that he wants to maintain the relaxed relational nature of such previous pairings, but also to 'build capacity' so that it is possible for many more students to benefit. FOCUS are initially focusing on four areas of influence: politics, business, career ministry and academia. They began by inviting twenty mentors and forty students to connect together, and have now added an annual mentoring conference and invited hundreds more graduates to join them. John is informally involved in the business track.

One of the key sources for new mentors was among the graduates of a FOCUS scheme called Short-Term Experience in Ministry (STEM), which blends intensive

---

[132] Statistics provided to me by FOCUS National Director George Ogalo August 2018. FOCUS was registered in Kenya in 1973 and affiliated with IFES in 1979.

training with the opportunity to spend a year as a volunteer FOCUS staff worker on campus or to serve with partner community development organizations. Well over 500 FOCUS graduates have passed through STEM since it was launched in 1992, and most are now building on what they learned through STEM by living out their faith in the workplace or in church-based ministry.[133] George tells me that some other IFES movements in the region have benchmarked the STEM programme in Kenya and started similar programmes in home countries such as Tanzania, Ethiopia, South Sudan and South Africa. When, a couple of years ago, FOCUS decided to begin more intentionally and systematically making use of its graduates in preparing students for the workplace, they invited STEM alumni to join the team as associate staff. George told me that it was simply a case of better using the human resources already in their sphere.

All of this is very new. George called FOCUS' mentoring scheme 'a pilot' and Susan, in our conversation, repeatedly used the words 'beginning to' as a preface to various aspects of her work. Each movement is attempting systematically to harness the swathes of quality graduates it has produced over the years.[134] OSCER and FOCUS have already, even without such a programme, impacted the church and workplace through folk like John, Adrian, Florin, Laurenţiu and Lucian, who have each maintained the missional posture of their student years as they began life in the

---

133 The exact figure is 547, according to what Mercy Waithira, current STEM coordinator for FOCUS, told me in September 2018.

134 ... as well as networking with others outside the movement who might be able to help: Susan, for example, regularly collaborates with 'Credinţă la Muncă' (Faith at Work), among others.

workplace and ministry through the local church. Their
graduates have been prepared for service in the wider world
by becoming accustomed, as Samuel Escobar says, to view
every context in which they find themselves as 'a mission
field'. But now the movements are going a step further
by readying students and graduates for the very unique
challenges of the specific professions or areas of society in
which they may find themselves.

BY THEIR GRADUATES YOU WILL KNOW THEM

A student movement's impact should be measured, in
part, by the quality of graduates it produces.[135] It should
be natural for students to enter the working world and
continue implementing the values and emphases they
learned while part of the Christian group on campus. They
can be aided in this, as we have seen, by ongoing input and
support from more experienced followers of Jesus who
have already worked through the specific challenges and
opportunities offered by various career paths. Christian
students sometimes express to me their openness to cross-
cultural mission by saying something like, 'I would love one
day to be able to serve God' or 'do something for God'. My
reply is usually, 'Why not do everything for him, starting
now?' We learn, live and speak for Jesus in our future
worlds by doing so in whatever one we now find ourselves.
Engaging the university, proclaiming Jesus there and
holistically addressing the most pressing questions of our
context, are valid in themselves and are also ways to prepare
Jesus' followers for the life ahead.

---

135 A thought I'm ninety-nine per cent sure I lifted – possibly *verbatim* – from
former IFES General Secretary Lindsay Brown.

While I rejoice and pray for Adrian's work among the second and third generation diaspora in Portland, as well as Florin's continued commitment to following Jesus in Canada, it's hard to avoid the sense that Romania – and other nations – suffer loss when their dynamic Christian leaders and a visionary businessmen of integrity relocate overseas: every dissatisfied emigrant is one less agent for change in their homeland. A student movement that can help its members prepare for daily engagement in an inhospitable system is a gift to its own nation as well as to the church. We don't want a world where nobody leaves – migration is a part of living in a globalized world and there will always be comings and goings from financial motivations as well as God's call – but as we build the mission team on campus, and continue investing in our members beyond graduation, the lights of the campus will also become the lights of entire nations.

QUESTIONS FOR REFLECTION OR DISCUSSION:

What values and practices encountered through your Christian student group, if you were or are part of one, are most applicable to the working world? How might they need (or have they needed) to be adapted for life after graduation?

In what ways do you see yourself tempted either to capitulate to the system or to flee from it? How does the challenge to 'take up your cross daily and follow me' apply to your situation? What concrete form does 'the cross' take for you?

Thinking about the pressures you just identified, how could you seek out Christian mentors experienced in this area? Is there someone you could contact to meet up with over coffee?

CHAPTER SIX:
MISSING FLAGS AND
BONELESS BUCKETS

TALES OF LEADERSHIP DEVELOPMENT
(SOLOMON ISLANDS AND MONGOLIA)

It began when nobody mentioned them. Their flag was not waved and their existence went unacknowledged. Among the crowd of wildly cheering students, six stood in silent shock. A discomfort, later described to me by several of the sextet as 'a holy jealousy', grew swiftly within each of them. They glanced across at one another and each knew instantly what the other was thinking. Within minutes, their incredulity gave way to action as one of them rose to their feet and unexpectedly addressed the room. Their words would have enormous effects reaching far beyond the borders of Viti Levu, the Fijian island where they were gathering.

The six were a long way from home. They'd grown up in the Solomon Islands. This cluster of six major islands and almost one-thousand smaller ones sits to the east of Papua New Guinea and the north-east of Australia. Lush palm-lined golden beaches and vibrant blue waters encircle most of its isles. Because of its relatively small population

– a little over half a million, according to the last census – the Solomon Islands partners together with eleven other Pacific island nations to operate a well-regarded research and tertiary teaching institution known as University of the South Pacific (USP). Each of the twelve nations hosts a campus specializing in specific areas of study. These six Solomon Islanders had relocated to Fiji to study ecology, and Vanuatu to study law.

For Darlcy, a law student in Vanuatu, moving away from the Solomons had been a transformative experience. She came from a nominally Christian family (many people in the South Pacific would self-identify as Christian) but this faith is often more a framework for ethical and family life than a live connection with God. One Solomon Islander explained his context to me: 'There's not a lot of Jesus for a country with so many churches.' And so it was only at university that Darlcy had begun to understand the concept of 'grace' – that God's welcome and acceptance comes to us as an unmerited gift achieved through the work of Jesus, and not as the product of our own virtue. She says that, over the course of her first year, this discovery re-coloured her relationship with God and enabled her to trust him for the first time. He moved from ethical reference point to encountered daily reality.

Darlcy first came across the idea of grace at a weekly Bible study of Emalus Christian Fellowship, the recently-founded student group which met on her campus. Each week they read a scriptural passage together and, under the guidance of the local staff worker Joel Atwood, they sought to apply it to their own lives. As Darlcy grew in understanding and experience of God through these studies, Joel and his successor Steve progressively gave her more responsibility in overseeing the group. They began to build a nucleus of student leaders who had come to study in Vanuatu from across the region. Tongans and Fijians were part of the team, so were two other Solomon Islanders – Godfrey and Richie. Joel and Steve, who successively pioneered the movement in Vanuatu, were working hard to make it sustainable for the long term. But, until now, their vision had not extended beyond Emalus Campus.

Joel and Steve were, therefore, as surprised as everyone else when the three Solomon Islanders from the Vanuatuan movement's student leadership team, along with three others, enrolled at USP's various Fijian campuses, stood up and expressed their 'holy jealousy'. The context was the South Pacific Regional Conference (SPARC), a triennial gathering for students from across the Pacific region of IFES.[136] An entire evening of the conference had been given over to prayer for the various student movements represented. When each nation was mentioned, students from that location rose to their feet, waved their flag and hollered in excitement, to the applause of everyone else in the room. They then shared the stories and challenges of their context and everybody prayed for them. Then the next country was highlighted and the process repeated. The six Solomon Islanders waited throughout the evening for their country to be named and when it eventually failed to occur, they all experienced the same simultaneous realization: there was no Christian student movement in the Solomon Islands.

Iulah, who was studying in Fiji, rose to her feet, and – speaking for the whole group – explained to the room

---

136 Specifically, the 2013 gathering.

that they had heard the stories and the work of God in all these other countries. Now, she said, they would love to see the same thing happen in their homeland. She asked if everybody could please pray for the universities and students of the Solomon Islands. Andy Shudall, then with the Tertiary Students Christian Fellowship (TSCF) in New Zealand, describes it as 'a remarkable moment'. He says that everyone present had the tangible sense of experiencing a crucial moment in God's mission among the universities. Nigel Pollock, then National Director of TCSF, stood with the students and led the gathering in prayer, drawing attention to the new thing God was doing. The time of prayer which followed was electric, and afterwards the six Solomon Islanders met with senior leaders of various student movements from around the region to plot a course forward.

Most of the students were a year or two away from graduation so the work in the Solomons wasn't about to start yet. Instead, they entered a period of preparation. Many of the movements around the region reached out to the six and purposely created opportunities for them to learn and develop. The Australian Fellowship of Evangelical Students (AFES), for example, invited them to come and attend their annual National Training Event free of charge, where they could attend practical seminars on aspects of campus ministry. They also had the chance at these conferences to spend several hours each day in intensive Bible study, as well as training to prepare and lead their own studies. This would prove critical in their future plans.

Godfrey and Iulah were the first to return home. They spent their initial few months, which fell during the summer break, enlisting a team who could work alongside them over the coming years. Their focus, throughout that summer, was on identifying and gathering Solomon Islanders home from their studies in overseas institutions for the holidays. Those interested were invited to prayer meetings for the universities, which they held in the open air under the trees on the lawns behind a local church. These increased in number each week until, soon, many locals were praying for the establishment of a Christian student movement in their country and the imaginations of numerous Solomon Islanders studying abroad were caught by the idea of coming home and assisting in the work.

Their next stop was to spend a year networking with church elders in order both to share the vision, and also to gain their input. Most pastors were supportive and several connected Godfrey and Iulah with students from their congregations. They also collectively suggested that Eric Maefonea, a local minister in the South Sea Evangelical Church, serve as a mentor and guide through the movement's early years. The original six, most of whom had now graduated and were permanently back in the Solomons, together with Eric and their now-enlarged network of returning overseas students, brought together the student contacts provided by local churches and began Bible studies on the USP campus. Following the model shown to them by Joel and Steve in Vanuatu, as well as through the AFES annual national training events and their experiences with the Fijian movement, they opened these discussions to their friends and advertised them around campus.

Soon many more, like Darlcy before them, were discovering the grace of Jesus through these studies. The movement – now named Solomon Islands Universities'

Christian Fellowship (SIUCF) – expanded to a second, smaller university – Solomon Islands International University – and their most recent national camp was attended by over one hundred students. This in a country with a total of just 4,000 undergraduate students. The 'holy jealousy' which ignited a mere year previously, when their flag was not present in a prayer meeting, had led to Christian communities thriving in the heart of two new universities and many more than six students living and speaking for Jesus at the heart of their campus.

STARTING FROM SCRATCH

The birth of SIUCF is an inspirational tale – six students irresistibly seized by a divine pull to return home and reach the universities of their homeland. But it would not be replicable in every context. Mongolia, for example, is said to have had just four known Christian believers in 1989.[137] It had, for the previous sixty-five years, been a state which officially rejected the existence of God and the free practice of religion. Unlike its neighbours, the USSR and China, where Christianity had been an established presence for several centuries prior to atheistic communist rule, no underground church had emerged during those years in Mongolia. There simply wasn't a Christian community from which it could have grown.

There had been brief moments in Mongolian history when Christianity flashed up on the radar, with the theologically-fringe Nestorian church gaining the strongest foothold and possibly having a presence as early as the

---

137 This figure is fairly widely cited, see: Jason Mandryk, *Operation World: The Definitive Prayer Guide to Every Nation* (IVP 2011), p.595.

500s, with several entire tribes having converted by the 1200s.[138] Many from the Nestorian Kerait tribe were among the political and military elite during the time of Chinggis (more commonly known as Genghis) Khan and his successors.[139] But all remnants of the faith have long since evaporated, save for some physical artefacts.[140] The default beliefs of most Mongolians were now some combination of atheistic materialism, Tibetan Buddhism and Shamanism. The latter is an ancient system of beliefs and practices centred on the spirit world and not dissimilar to animism or some forms of paganism. Most people in Mongolia knew almost nothing of Jesus and the Christian faith.

When the nation transitioned to democracy in the early 1990s there emerged, for the first time in many centuries, an opening for outside Christians to come and share Jesus. Daehoon Park, a former staff member with the South Korean IFES movement (InterVarsity Fellowship; IVF), was one of the first to arrive. He took a position as philosophy lecturer at the International University of Ulaanbaatar and, as he made friends on campus, he also began a series of small group Bible studies for those interested in finding out

138 I say 'fringe', but the conventional understanding is that they were actually outright heretical in their views of Jesus' nature; Nestorians were separated from the wider church in the 400s after their views were condemned at both the First Council of Ephesus and the Council of Chalcedon. The largest present-day descendent of the Nestorian church is the Assyrian Church of the East, which mostly exists within the Middle East. It should be noted that the accuracy of our current historical understanding of what Nestorians believed is currently a matter of academic debate. For the timeline of Mongolian Christianity: Mark A. Lamport (ed.), *Encyclopedia of Christianity in the Global South* (Rowman & Littlefield, 2018), pp.536-537.

139 Timothy May (ed.), *The Mongol Empire: A Historical Encyclopedia* (ABC-CLIO, 2017), p.230.

140 James C.Y. Watt, *The World of Khubilai Khan: Chinese Art in the Yuan Dynasty* (Yale University Press, 2010), pp.30-33.

more about his Christian faith. A hub of thirty Mongolian students become followers of Jesus as a result and began meeting regularly to read the Bible with Park. They called themselves the Fellowship of Christian Students (FCS).

Saikhanaa, a student at the time, told me that she came from an atheistic family and was invited by a friend to begin attending the events Park was organizing. She came with a whole stack of questions and objections, and was surprised to find people willing to sit and explore them with her at length. They also invited her to join a Bible discussion and, through this, she came to understand better the message of Jesus. When she eventually committed her life to him, she received more than just encouragement. The longer-standing converts of the group, to whom Park had now given some leadership responsibility, also offered her practical help in living out her faith.

One particularly memorable experience was their challenge to come to the apartment Park was now renting for the students and, at 6am each morning for thirty days, spend an hour in prayer and reading the Bible with five others. The whole Bible, in fact, had only just been translated into the Mongolian language for the first time and so she was among the first in her nation to immerse themselves in it. Saikhanaa says that, by the end of the month, the experience had ingrained in her a habit of daily personal time with God which continues even sixteen years later. Saikhanaa explained to me that Park created a structured series of such experiences, which were designed to walk students from first contact with Jesus through to leading evangelistic Bible studies and cell groups for themselves.

Park eventually left Ulaanbaatar after four years of pioneering work, just as his former IVF Korea colleague

Seung Hoon Lee – along with former IVCF USA staff Tom and Nancy Lin – arrived to assist with the development of FCS. Seung Hoon Lee recalled to me that he was delighted to meet the small hub of students Park had gathered. Lee knew that not long ago – even as recently as his own student years – Mongolia had been home to just four known Christian believers.[141] But by the time he moved to Ulaanbaatar – less than a decade after democracy had emerged in Mongolia – there were many more.[142] Thanks to the efforts of Daehoon Park, and the work of God through him, they were greeted not only by new believers, but also by four graduates of FCS who had been selected to become the very first full time staff members of the Mongolian student movement. Each

---

[141] When Lee graduated from university, Mongolia (indeed anywhere across the sea) was far from his mind. His graduation plans were pretty simple – he wanted to join the staff of InterVarsity Fellowship (IVF) in his native South Korea and to help pioneer a new student group in the Korean city of Gwangju. The first time Mongolia even flickered across Lee's consciousness was towards the end of his first year on staff. Lindsay Brown, then the General Secretary of IFES, visited to give a series of talks for IVF staff. In one of his messages he described the situation in Mongolia and suggested that Korean Christians – with their linguistic and cultural similarities to Mongolians – would be the ideal pioneers for a new student movement based in the capital city of Ulaanbaatar. Over the following two years Lee felt himself consistently being tugged towards involvement in mission beyond his homeland. It was little things – a message by visiting speaker John Stott, a biography of pioneer missionary James Hudson Taylor, being given responsibility for the global mission seminar track at IVF's national conference – which each seemed to ignite something in him. A definite and undeniable pull was emerging. At the end of his third year on staff, at the age of twenty-five, Lee made a public commitment to God that he was willing to serve overseas.

[142] Mongolia became a multi-party state following a peaceful revolution in 1990, with the communist Mongolian People's Republic formally ending in 1992. The Mongolian People's Revolutionary Party, the ruling party under communism, won early elections in Mongolia before being voted out in 1996, and then returning through popular vote to power – either alone or in coalition – at various points thereafter.

was from a Buddhist or atheistic family and had come to faith through their contact with Park and the students in whom he had invested. Saikhanaa was one of them.

The new team of Lee, Tom and Nancy didn't see their job as replacing Park. In their minds, the initial phase of 'pioneering' was done. The next stage, they hoped, was to be one of 'settlement'; their challenge was how to shape this small community of believers and fledgling staff team they had inherited into a sustainable Mongolian-led student movement.

THE PERPETUAL PIONEERS

The challenge facing Lee, Tom and Nancy was not a unique one. A student movement inevitably endures or folds based on its leadership development. Unlike churches, which can limp on for many years after they lose the habit of developing younger believers into capable stewards of the work, a student movement automatically graduates up to a third of its membership every year. Cambridge University Inter-Collegiate Christian Union, founded in 1877 and the oldest local group within IFES, changes its student leadership team every year. That means they have needed over one hundred and fifty leadership transitions in their history.[143] Swiftly and effectively developing leaders is the only way to prevent total collapse – or, at the very least, loss of direction – within a very short time scale.

Such transfers are not only part of the DNA of any student movement. They are also built into the foundations

---

143 I owe this observation to former UCCF General Secretary Oliver Barclay: Oliver Barclay, *From Cambridge to the World: 125 Years of Student Witness* (IVP, 2002) p.11.

of the church. Jesus, when he physically departed from his followers a few weeks after his resurrection, left a fairly small nub of committed friends. Just 120 gathered to pray in the days before Pentecost.[144] When one considers that over 500 people saw Jesus physically risen, many thousands ate a meal they saw him spectacularly produce from just a handful of fish and bread, and seemingly half the capital city had raucously acclaimed him as king just a few weeks previously, then 120 seems like a pitifully small crowd.[145]

The leading lights of this small and fragile community had mostly fled for safety the moment Jesus was arrested. One of them ran naked into the night when a soldier grabbed his robe,[146] Peter managed to spend the night of the crucifixion swearing and lying his way out of trouble,[147] the rest had an even more nondescript weekend hiding out while their master was tried, tortured, killed and buried.[148] Thomas' faith in Jesus so completely collapsed that he struggled to believe even when Jesus physically turned up alive in the same room. Yet it was to this unimpressive band that Jesus handed the earthly leadership of his movement when he departed. There has never been a sharper drop in quality between two generations of leaders.

Jesus' ascension, surprisingly, did not trigger a further downturn in the fortunes of the church. Against all expectation, it exploded. It only took a few days until Peter – the foul-mouthed liar who abandoned Jesus just

---

144 Acts 1:15.

145 Matthew 14:13–21, Matthew 21:1–11, 1 Corinthians 15:6.

146 Mark 14:51–52.

147 Mark 14:66–72.

148 Interestingly, while Jesus' male friends mostly abandoned him, his female ones seemed to stay close throughout his dying hours and beyond.

over a month previously – gave a bold speech in the heart of Jerusalem, resulting in the movement expanding by several thousand in a single afternoon. Within a few short years, many major cities of the Eastern Roman Empire, including the cultural capitals of Rome and Athens, were home to communities of Jesus followers.[149] Africa had its first convert and Paul was making plans for Spain, then the western edge of the known world.[150] A hundred years later there were churches in most major port cities of the Mediterranean – African, Asian and European[151] – and by the end of the second century it seems that churches were springing up as far afield as South India.[152]

It's an incredible tale of multiplication. Yet, when we scour the narratives of Jesus' life, we don't find him preoccupied with instructing others in the technical minutiae of organizational development. We observe, in fact, relatively little of what today passes for leadership training. Jesus mostly seems to be hanging out and talking with his friends. They spend much of their time simply conversing over dinner or during lengthy walks between cities. It consistently seems like he was more interested in teaching them to know and love God than he was in giving

---

[149] See the book of Romans and Acts 17:16–34.

[150] Acts 8:26–39, Romans 15:24, Romans 15:28.

[151] Stark, *Cities of God*.

[152] Many Indian Christians claim the apostle Thomas founded their church in AD 69 and was martyred four years later. Since Jewish communities existed on the Indian coast long before Jesus' birth, and there was a second major wave of immigration to India from Israel after the AD 70 destruction of Jerusalem, it's not an outrageous claim. At the very least there were certainly well-established Christian communities in India by the 200s. See: Robert Eric Frykenberg, *Christianity in India: From Beginnings to the Present* (Oxford University Press, 2013), p.101, p.103, & p.115.

them tricks and tips for successful management. It's not that Jesus is being spontaneous – it's actually very difficult to read the gospels and come away with the idea that he ever acted without intent or forethought – but more that he prioritizes their learning to live as children of God over learning executive skills.[153]

When the time comes for Jesus' physical departure, he uses a couple of striking words in relation to his followers' ongoing mission. The first is 'witnesses': he tells them they will be his 'witnesses in Jerusalem, and in all Judea and Samaria, and the ends of the earth'.[154] A witness is a person who has experienced something and is willing to communicate that to others. They are someone 'who knows the truth and can testify before a court of law, declaring what [they have] seen or heard'.[155] Jesus doesn't say 'you will be my managers' – he sees the heart of their capacity to live and speak for him as being a first-hand encounter with himself, both his life and his words.[156]

---

153 Even when Jesus directly addressed the issue of leadership, he didn't simply focus on technique. Commenting on Roman models of management, he said: 'You know that the rulers of the Gentiles lord it over them, and their high officials exercise authority over them. Not so with you. Instead, whoever wants to become great among you must be your servant, and whoever wants to be first must be your slave – just as the Son of Man did not come to be served, but to serve, and to give his life as a ransom for many.' (Matthew 20:25–28). After washing his friends' sweaty feet at the end of a long day he said: 'You call me "Teacher" and "Lord", and rightly so, for that is what I am. Now that I, your Lord and Teacher, have washed your feet, you also should wash one another's feet. I have set you an example that you should do as I have done for you.' (John 13:13–15).

154 Acts 1:8.

155 Joel B. Green, Scot McKnight & I. Howard Marshall (eds.), *Dictionary of Jesus and the Gospels* (IVP, 1992), p.877.

156 There certainly is something unique about the 'witness' of those who were with Jesus in the flesh over several years. But everyone who has experienced God's work in their lives is also, according to the author of Hebrews, a 'witness' (Hebrews 12:1).

Jesus also instructs them to 'make disciples'.[157] Discipleship, in the first century, was the practice of a more experienced teacher taking on one or several pupils who would be with them and learn from them, that they might adopt their master's teaching and way of life.[158] It was common practice among both Jewish rabbis and Greek philosophers to take on disciples, though Jesus gave the whole practice his own personal twist.[159] Interestingly, when Jesus told his followers to 'make disciples', he didn't define *how* they should do so. As his disciples they should already know: he was really saying, 'What I did with you, go and do with others.'

It's often observed that Jesus implemented discipleship on four levels: 'the crowds', the seventy-two, the Twelve and then his inner circle of three – Peter, James and John.[160] Each one receives a different degree of input. The crowds – which include everyone who turned up or tagged along – get to hear the classic teachings like the Sermon on the Mount and many of the parables, as well as witness his interactions with Jewish leaders and his healings. He also has frequent interpersonal encounters with a whole range of individuals, so the wider community's experience of Jesus was far from limited to listening to him teach. From among these crowds, presumably, came some of the 120 who met and prayed between the Ascension and Pentecost.

---

157 Matthew 28:19.

158 D.R.W. Wood, *New Bible Dictionary* (IVP, 1996), p.277.

159 Wood, *New Bible Dictionary*, p.277; Green, McKnight & Marshall, *Dictionary of Jesus and the Gospels*, p.877.

160 See, for example: Robert E. Coleman, *The Masterplan of Evangelism* (Spire, 2010). Some manuscripts read 'seventy-two' while others read 'seventy'. For our purposes here it doesn't matter too much which is accurate.

The seventy-two tantalizingly flicker before our eyes in the briefest of stories, where Jesus sends them off with his authority to heal, exorcise and speak of him.[161] On their return he listens to their reports and helps them to interpret their experience in the light of God's nature and the scriptural narrative. They have been handed additional duties in his movement and provided with both prior training and orientation into Jesus' preferred methodology, as well as receiving a time of debriefing with him. Early church tradition holds that the seventy-two became pioneers of Christianity across the Roman world; Barnabas, Thaddaeus, Sosthenes and Matthias – all names familiar from the New Testament – were said to have been part of this group.[162]

The Twelve, likewise, are given escalating levels of responsibility by Jesus and even closer contact with him: after Jesus' public conversations and teachings, he frequently spends time alone with them, helping them process what they have witnessed. They, unlike the crowds or the seventy-two, are his most constant companions throughout the four gospels.

The three, who were also part of the Twelve, were sometimes called upon to be with Jesus at crucial moments like the transfiguration or his agonized pre-crucifixion prayer session in the garden.[163] They, unsurprisingly, seem to be at the forefront of the early chapters of Acts. And so, though Jesus' teaching and character is consistent

---

161 Luke 10:1–24.

162 Eusebius, the fourth-century historian, cited in: Arthur A. Just Jr. (ed.), *Ancient Christian Commentary on Scripture: New Testament III, Luke* (IVP, 2003), p.171.

163 Mark 9:2–13, 14:32–42.

regardless of the company or situation, he also deliberately 'proportioned his life to those he wanted to train';[164] 'Other things being equal', writes Robert Coleman, 'the more concentrated the size of the group being taught, the greater the opportunity for effective instructions'.[165]

When vacancies later arise for community oversight – which they very swiftly do after the Ascension – it is from the pool of existing 'witnesses' and 'disciples' that individuals are selected. Matthias, for example, is able to step into Judas' place because he has 'been with ... Jesus ... beginning from John's baptism to the time when Jesus was taken up'.[166] He must have been part of either the seventy-two or the crowds; he clearly didn't pop out of nowhere.[167] When – not long thereafter – complaints about the distribution of food among the church's widows lead to the formation of a finance and logistics team to deal with various internal matters, the community again reaches beyond the twelve and chooses 'seven men ... who are known to be full of the Spirit and wisdom'.[168] This selecting from among the disciples and witnesses continues right through to Paul's final letters, where he emphasizes the character of overseers – expressed in their family life, willingness to extend hospitality and financial dealings – just as much as, if not more than, their capacity to preach.[169]

Leadership development, then, is an extension of disciple-making. A student movement which consistently

---

164 Coleman, *The Master Plan of Evangelism*, p.26.
165 Ibid.
166 Acts 1:21–22.
167 Church tradition holds he was one of the seventy-two.
168 Acts 6:3.
169 1 Timothy 3:1–13, Titus 1:6–9.

seeks to grow people who love Jesus, know the Scriptures and put their faith into practice will never be short of potential leaders. Darlcy, Godfrey, Iulah and Saikhanaa learned to follow Jesus through Bible studies and practical instruction in the basics of following Jesus, as led by Joel, Steve and Park. For Darlcy and Saikhanaa, neither of whom had a relationship with God prior to university, this was their initiation into the way of Jesus. And for all of them, their first years as students were a time of developing as 'witnesses', or people who had experienced Jesus for themselves, knew his words, and were prepared to make a public stand for him.

THE BURNING PLAN

When Seung Hoon Lee and the Lins arrived in Ulaanbaatar, their intent was to follow Jesus' example by preparing younger leaders for their future physical departure. Their aim was to cultivate witnesses and disciples. They decided, almost as soon as their initial language study had ended, that it would make most strategic sense to split the group into several smaller communities. Each was to focus on a single campus and would be supported by either Tom or Lee. They rented two extra apartments around the city, along with maintaining the lease on a central location contracted by Park when campus access issues had prevented FCS from holding explicitly Christian meetings at the university, and each group used one of them as a place for hospitality, prayer and Bible study.

Tom told me that one of their priorities was to formulate simple and replicable ways of developing student leaders which could be refined by future generations of Mongolian leaders. Whereas, in his previous and future campus ministry roles with IVCF in the United States, he valued an array of methods, each with its own subtle nuances, Tom says that the Mongolian situation called for a single, more standardized approach which could easily be understood and re-implemented by leaders who had mostly been Christians for only a few years. They therefore took a three-step pattern already established by Park, and ensured that every new believer firstly joined a study in the basics of the Bible, secondly spent a year participating in a cell group where they learned how to pray and live as a follower of Jesus in community, and then thirdly – if showing growth as a follower of Jesus – began training to lead their own FCS cell group. This basic structure was augmented by a range of other activities and training events, including conferences and camps.

Shagai, one of Tom and Lee's earliest new Mongolian contacts, typifies the FCS path to leadership. He had become a student at the Mongolian University of Science and Technology in Ulaanbaatar just as Tom and Lee arrived in the country. Christianity was unknown to him, having grown up somewhere on the intersection between Buddhism and Shamanism. His grandmother was custodian to the family's set of idols and sacred fetishistic totems which, it was believed, possessed protective spiritual power. Some of his earliest childhood memories are of her teaching him a secret formula of ancient Tibetan words he could use whenever evil forces or a sense of darkness assailed him during the night time. Even today he can still repeat the phrase, which is merely a fragment from entire books of such lines which are memorized by many Mongolian monks.

Shagai, on arrival at university, was already asking questions about the picture of reality with which he had grown up. He soon became friends, whilst still a teenage undergraduate, with a classmate who invited him to weekly meetings in one of FCS' three apartments. He was amazed by what he witnessed. An emphasis on spiritual reality was nothing new for him. But to see it accompanied by a welcoming and loving community – and a genuine lack of fear in the face of the unseen realm – was something entirely new for Shagai. He remembers nothing of the message preached that day, but after only a few weeks he decided to investigate the source of these students' spiritual vibrancy and accepted the invitation to join an investigative Bible discussion. Within six months he had opened his life to Jesus. The Bible discussion which catalyzed Shagai's conversion was led by a Park-era convert from Buddhism, Tsetsgee, who – just a few years later and while still only in her twenties – would go on to die from cancer. She remains a poignant reminder of the impact we can have even if the years given to us are few. Many she introduced to Jesus are still a part of the movement in some form or another.

Shagai, after meeting Jesus through Tsetsgee, followed the three-stage path designed by Park and developed by Lee and Tom. He was invited to join a study in biblical essentials, then spent a year as a member of a student small group, and then – once Tom and Lee were confident that Shagai had laid some basic foundations for a life of following Jesus – was selected by them for training as a cell group leader, who could himself invest in and develop new followers of Jesus according to the same patterns he had experienced. In total it took less than two years for Shagai to move from complete ignorance of Jesus to a position of Christian leadership. Soon thereafter he was invited to work full time with FCS and became the first of the post-Park era converts to assume a staff position.

Whilst Tom and Lee had already inherited from Park this workable model for student leadership development, they did not yet have any systems in place for training new staff such as Shagai. Innovation would be necessary. Drawing on their own beneficial experiences of residential staff training in the US and South Korea respectively, Tom and Lee invited new staff to spend three months living in one of the FCS apartments. During this time, they would work alongside Tom and Lee with students on campus and also in the FCS apartments. They would also receive daily teaching sessions on topics such as 'how to preach', 'leading Bible study', 'Old Testament survey', 'New Testament survey', 'systematic theology', 'Christian character', 'spiritual formation', 'cults', 'apologetics' and – space here does not permit the full list, so check the footnotes – pretty much everything needed for a new staff worker.[170]

Alongside the development of staff, they also worked on the movement's legal and financial structures: during Shagai's time on staff, FCS became registered as an international NGO, thus simplifying administrative

---

170 The full list from the 2005 New Staff Training, as sent to me by Tom Lin, includes: Relationship With Other Staff, Support-Raising, Bible Interpretation, English Grammar, Old Testament Survey, Leading Bible Study, Maintaining Our Life, Christian Leadership, One-To-One, Evangelism, Apologetics / Defending Your Faith, How To Lead Small Groups, How To Preach, Making Disciples, Systematic Theology, Christian Leadership, Mongol Culture: Old And New Ways, Shamanism, Secularism And Buddhism, Cost & Joy of a Disciplemaker's Life, What Is Worship?, Christian Dating, Church History, Christian Character, Local Church And Mission Agency, New Testament Survey, Philosophy Of FCS Movement, Counselling, Time Management, Spiritual Formation, Inner-Healing, Management, Mission, IFES Student Movements, Spiritual Warfare, Cults (Mormons, Moonies, etc.) and Listening.

aspects of the work such as employment and finances. The movement's three apartments were replaced by a single large office occupying the top floor of a two-storey dark green 1920s apartment complex located centrally to several Ulaanbaatar campuses. It was here, a few minutes' walk from the spectacular Museum of Mongolian Dinosaurs, that Tom and Lee – along with their soon-to-be successor Barnabas – sketched out a four-year plan to switch FCS from missionary co-leadership to full local leadership, with Mongolian Christians expected to take over every aspect of the work, from running the NGO to developing new staff. None of the three missionaries felt Shagai and his colleagues, being such relatively new converts, were yet ready for this responsibility and they wanted to prepare them thoroughly.

The forty-eight-month transition period began in January 2008, shortly after Tom's departure, and commenced smoothly. But within a few weeks it had crashed in a burning heap when local police raided their weekly meeting and arrested all the leaders. The office lease was instantly cancelled, their international NGO was declared illegal and both Lee and Barnabas were deported. The only way to continue, they were told, was if they registered as a local (rather than international) NGO and this would legally require an exclusively Mongolian staff team and board. No foreigners were to hold any position in the organization.

Neither Tom, Lee nor Barnabas anticipated this transition happening for at least another four years. But now it was forced upon them and so Shagai became the first ever Mongolian General Secretary of FCS, six years after his own conversion and nine years since Park launched the first evangelistic student Bible studies in the city.

NOT GOING TO SCHOOL IN A BUCKET

When FCS was suddenly transformed into a fully Mongolian-led movement, nobody, foreigner nor local, thought they were ready. But, amazingly and despite the unexpectedly jolting circumstances of the transition, the young movement – managed and led entirely by relatively new converts – continued to grow in strength. There are now FCS groups in five different faculties and the leadership are planning to send one of their senior staff members to the west of the country so she can pioneer their first ever group located outside the capital city. Five or six FCS graduates even teach at the International University of Ulaanbaatar, where Park – as professor of philosophy – first initiated the movement.

When Lee and Barnabas eventually re-entered the country, their roles had changed. Barnabas told me that whereas Park's era was one of 'pioneering' and Tom and Lee's was a time of 'settlement', they now entered a new era of 'partnership', where foreign Christians acted as advisors and coaches but no longer drove the work forward. This had always been the eventual aim: Tom, Lee and Barnabas all viewed their role in the leadership of FCS as temporary. Each, when I spoke to them, told me that from the outset their purpose had been to work themselves out of a job. Even today, most of FCS' leadership say that they would have preferred the smoother four-year transition period between foreign and local leadership. But, despite the handover not occurring as straightforwardly as originally hoped, they still thrived.

Perhaps one reason for this lies in Tom and Lee's focus on creating simple, replicable structures for leadership development and the growth of disciples. It provided Shagai and his successors with something they could easily re-implement even when those who created the arrangement departed; FCS cell leader and new staff development still continues, albeit in an ever-evolving form, to follow these early patterns. It is very easy to dismiss the value of such carefully-designed systems. Many Christians, in fact, assume that structure is the enemy of true spiritual life, which – they intuit – should really be marked by spontaneity and complete openness.

Whenever I hear this kind of perspective, my mind flashes back to one of my earliest childhood memories. My older sister Rebecca, returning from school and presumably fresh from a fascinating biology lesson on the human body, posed me a question: 'Do you know what would happen if you didn't have a skeleton?' I had no idea and asked her for the answer. 'You would have to go to school,' she told me dramatically, 'in a bucket'. The picture of my collapsed, boneless organism peering out of a blue plastic pail, perhaps carried daily to class by my mother, appealed to my boyhood love of the absurd and grotesque and remained ingrained in my imagination. I repeated it to all my friends on the playground the next day.

Rebecca's comment probably wasn't intended as a metaphor for organizational development, but the observation underlying it is relevant for all Christian student movements; structure, like a skeleton, can actually enable life to flourish. We can all point to examples of church or organizational structures which hinder missional vibrancy, but the occasional – or even frequent – existence of unhealthy skeletons doesn't mean the rest of us should de-bone ourselves. Tom and Lee, by adapting

Park's path to discipleship and augmenting it with a staff training program and healthy governance and financial management practices, had put in place the osseous matter which enabled the Mongolian student movement to walk and then run.

As we have seen, FCS very nearly collapsed due to structural issues: its initial constitution as an international NGO caused ruptures with the government and led them to lose leases on all the properties where they met. It would be easy, as an outsider, to idealistically advise FCS to continue as an informal and underground movement. But, in reality, lack of legal status – along with their campus access issues – would render it impossible to employ staff or obtain a meeting place larger than an individual's small apartment. It could doubtless survive, but with many more restrictions than before. So the establishment of a local NGO enabled them to order their financial affairs and obtain an office space where they could train and develop the next generation of students and staff.

In the Solomon Islands, structure was a priority from the outset. Many student movements start through one or two particularly charismatic individuals with a knack for gathering people and achieving much with few resources. They temporarily provide the initial skeleton to the movement. Daehoon Park in Mongolia, Steve Gibb and Joel Atwood in Vanuatu and Godfrey Male and Iulah Pitamama in the Solomon Islands are five examples from this chapter. When they leave, there either needs to be some kind of intentional plan for ongoing ossification or the movement may collapse back into its bucket. Godfrey had witnessed this first hand after Steve and Joel left Vanuatu and the movement temporarily found itself feeling adrift without their firm direction. He was determined to avoid this situation in the Solomon Islands.

Godfrey had witnessed how the work in Vanuatu steadied partly because of input from Howard Spencer, a decades-long veteran of AFES in Australia. Howard visited and helped students, staff and volunteers think through some basic questions like 'what is our vision?' and 'what can we put in place to keep this going?' Together, over the course of several days, they designed a structure which enabled the movement to operate in the longer-term. Godfrey and his colleagues in the Solomon Islands invited Howard to do the same just one year after they began their first Bible studies. His input was invaluable.

One result of Howard's visit was the establishment of a local board, comprised of eight Solomons-based individuals. Their role would be to keep SIUCF true to its vision and also to ensure it had a financial development plan. Darlcy was appointed Treasurer and Godfrey the Assistant Chairperson. Separate from the board is a team of five volunteer staff who all have regular jobs in areas like law, business or government. They commit to sustaining the work on campus through hands-on mentoring, advice and input into student Bible studies.

The separation of board, who handle big picture and organizational development, and volunteer staff, who engage in direct work with students, has been tremendously helpful. Darlcy told me that it helps everybody know their role and ensures that each area of the work is covered adequately. The staff are free to do their Scripture-based interpersonal work without worrying about the logistics of running an NGO. Likewise, the wisdom and expertise of local SIUCF graduates and supporters is not lost when they graduate – they help the organization grow without pressure to be part of daily work on campus.

Howard told me that structural issues are probably the main reason young movements struggle to grow. Having a leadership development plan, like Tom and Lee developed in Mongolia, is essential to keeping the work going through multiple generations of students. This, harnessed to a carefully-designed set of management and governance arrangements, are the bones which keep a movement out of the bucket.

VITAL FOR ALL

Leadership development, then, has been crucial in enabling fragile young movements to survive and flourish. Those who pioneered work in Mongolia and the Solomon Islands made the identification and preparation of their successors a priority. They crafted imitable and adaptable practices which have become absorbed by those who followed, and both FCS and SIUCF continue to endure and expand because each new generation is committed to readying the following one. They do this firstly by cultivating a pool of disciples and witnesses who can live and speak for Jesus on campus, and then, secondly, by selecting some from among them for more intensive input and increased responsibility.

The rapid turnover of the student population, with up to a third of an institution graduating each year, means that leadership development is essential not only for new movements; even longstanding ones will rapidly stagnate and lose missional focus if they don't retain and refresh this emphasis. Those of us who can look back and celebrate God's work over decades in our own contexts must be wary of complacently assuming that things will continue smoothly just because they have always done so. Campus ministry is a task of perpetual pioneering and its sustainability rests, in part, upon constantly investing afresh in the growth of new students and staff. It is this accent which enabled six students to move from distress over a missing flag to planting new Christian communities in the universities of their homeland.

QUESTIONS FOR REFLECTION OR DISCUSSION:

Can you discern how leadership development happens in your context? What occurs to identify and cultivate new leaders for the movement, both locally and nationally?

Think about the areas in which you have responsibility, whether in the student movement or in the rest of life (home, work, family, volunteering or elsewhere). In what concrete ways does your growth to this point as a 'disciple' and 'witness' help you in those?

Are there other Christians in whom you could begin investing time and energy to help develop them as Jesus' followers? How, practically, could you do that? If you're not sure, who has experience in this area and could advise you?

CHAPTER SEVEN:
HOSTILE PLACARDS AND
EMPTY FUEL TANKS

TALES OF FINANCIAL SUSTAINABILITY
(SOUTH KOREA AND BURKINA FASO)

He didn't say a word and simply stared at the ground. His face was the very model of studied inexpression. Was he embarrassed, shy, angry, indifferent or something else? It was hard for her to tell. She stepped towards him, reached for his outstretched arm and took the card. The big English words, written in red and white against a glossy black background, read simply, 'No Thanks'. The 'T' was styled like a cross – she could see that from the moment he'd flicked it in her direction – but everything else was scripted far smaller in *Hangul*, the Korean alphabet. She took it from his hand and, looking more closely, slowly read the words:

> *We have no religion.*
> *If you break through the fence of brainwashing and look around at the world you will see that God did not make man:*
> *Man made religion.*
> *You can learn more inspiringly:*
> *We do not harm other people.*
> *You should live quietly with the certainties of faith.*

There is very little to blame.
So please do not bother us.[171]

As she processed the words she looked up to ask him for more details. But he had gone. It wasn't long before the experience had repeated itself. By the end of the day, when she got back together with her friends, she discovered that many of them had been met with silent students sheepishly extending a 'No Thanks' card in their direction.[172]

It was a dry week in late February, when the cards flooded campus. The students of InterVarsity Fellowship (IVF) consider it one of the two most important weeks of the year. South Korea has one of the most famously rigorous educational systems in the world and new students can expect their time at university to be, if nothing else, intense once lectures kick off in March. But it doesn't begin that way: in most universities, the first fourteen days on campus are a flurry of social activities intended to provide freshmen with a web of social connections across the institution. IVF, like many IFES movements around the world, use this time as an opportunity to invite new students to join their group. Other Christian groups do the same. So, in fact, do most non-religious groups, from basketball and football through to financial and political societies. It's the natural time to do so.

Later, IVF discover that the card was produced by a group of Korean students calling themselves 'Freethinkers'. They

---

[171] My thanks to IVF staff worker Sung Woo Kim for his help in translating the card, and other words, from this article: Byung Wang, 대학가에 '전도, 노 땡큐!' 카드 확산, NewsNNet, May 23 2017, http://m.newsnnet.com/news/articleView.html?idxno=4920, (Accessed 28 March 2019). I made some adjustments, for ease of readability, to his original translation.

[172] This opening section is an imaginative retelling of the event, which was described to me by Jongho Kim of IVF Korea, who also read and approved what I wrote here.

made the cards to help new students avoid conversation with Christian groups on campus. If someone were to approach them then they could simply hold up the card and keep their lips shut. They distributed them widely and made them known on social media. When I contacted Freethinkers to ask them about the project, I was informed that it was a 'preach refusal card', designed to 'politely and simply notify our intention to refuse Christians' advances'.[173] The card was not a response to IVF specifically, who tend to be more respectful than the groups cited in media reports, but nevertheless they too found themselves confronted by this wall of silence.[174]

HOW TO BECOME UNPOPULAR

The 'No Thanks' sign was not an isolated event. It was part of a wider national backlash against the evangelical movement in South Korea. A series of financial scandals involving prominent Korean megachurches started the rot. But the negativity really went viral after twenty-three Korean missionaries were kidnapped by the Taliban in Afghanistan and held hostage. The crisis dominated local media for over a month until the South Korean government

---

[173] Interestingly, the person with whom I corresponded at Freethinkers told me that they *want* to discuss religion on campus. But they perceive many Christian groups as being characterized by aggressive 'don't take "no" for an answer' style tactics. They told me: 'The problem is, that they usually do not accept our refusal at all, and hold us up until they speak all thing [sic] they planned to speak'. If this current chapter were on evangelism, this would be rich material for considering how Christians around the world (and I'm not referring to IVF here, at all) often miss the open doors before them and default to ineffective received methodologies which, while marked by an admirable passion, are not perceived as intended by those outside the Christian community.

[174] See: Wang, 대학가에 '전도, 노 땡큐!' 카드 확산, http://m.newsnnet.com/news/articleView.html?idxno=4920.

eventually agreed to withdraw all its peacekeeping troops from the country in exchange for the release of its citizens.

Many Koreans saw the incident as having publically humiliated their nation for the sake of a handful of evangelicals who – it was perceived – were self-indulgently taking risks for their religion. It was also rumoured, though not substantiated, that over twenty million dollars was paid to the Taliban as part of the negotiation process. Evangelicals had therefore become a source of national shame and were also viewed as an inadvertent trigger for Korean taxpayers funding Islamic fundamentalism.[175]

It was a new position for South Korean Christians. They had long held a special place in the life of their nation.[176] Some writers describe the twentieth-century history of Korea as a quest for 'national salvation' and, at every turn, evangelicals were seen to be on the side of the liberators. Back in the 1920s, when evangelicals still constituted just one per cent of the Korean population, many of them played a disproportionately prominent role in protesting the abuses of the occupying Japanese military during a brutal colonization which lasted over two decades. A fifth of all people arrested as political prisoners by the Japanese were evangelical.[177] The most famous of these was a student called Chung Jae-yong who, in 1919, launched the (peaceful) resistance movement by bravely reading a Korean

---

175 Saeed Ali Achakzai, 'South Korea Paid $20 million ransom: Taliban leader', *Reuters*, 1 September 2007, https://www.reuters.com/article/us-afghan-koreans-ransom/south-korea-paid-20-million-ransom-taliban-leader-idUSCOL31793120070901, (Accessed 28 March 2019).

176 The following sketch of Korean evangelical history and the specific statistics cited are my summary, drawing upon: Timothy Lee, *Born Again: Evangelicalism in Korea* (University of Hawaii Press: 2010), as well as information and perspectives supplied to me by Jongho Kim of IVF.

177 Lee, *Born Again* p.39.

declaration of independence to a crowd of thousands of protestors – soon to be violently attacked by the rapidly-approaching Japanese police – in central Seoul.

Japanese rule ended in 1945 and new threats emerged. The 1948 general election saw the North of the country vote for communist Kim Il Sung and the South for right-wing Syngman Rhee. Each man formed their own government and claimed the right to govern the whole Korean peninsula. Brutal repression of those perceived to be sympathetic to the other government was common. Tens of thousands were massacred by both Sung and Rhee's troops, and evangelicals – who now made up two per cent of the Korean population – were frequently on the receiving end of Northern brutality. It was common for the communists to dig 'cavernous holes in the ground and [bury] alive ministers, elders, deacons, and other Christians along with hundreds of other citizens'.[178]

Almost half of Northern evangelicals fled south for safety before, and during, the ensuing civil war, abandoning the Northern capital of Pyongyang – once dubbed 'The Jerusalem of the East' because of how many Christians lived there – and began spreading the Christian faith to those around them. Once again, in the eyes of many South Koreans, evangelicals had been against the oppressors in the collective struggle for their national liberation.

Evangelicalism in the South was reinvigorated by the Northern refugees. By 1950 as many as ninety per cent of new Southern churches were planted by freshly-settled Northerners. Soon IVF, under the leadership of General Secretary Samuel Yoon – one-time death row prisoner

---

178 Lee, *Born Again*, p.68

of the North Korean army – joined IFES.[179] They found an increasing openness to their message. Over the next thirty years, evangelicalism more than doubled in size each decade and by 1985, a quarter of all South Koreans were evangelical believers. The country had by this time become home to the largest Pentecostal church in the world (the then 350,000-member Yoido Full Gospel Church), the largest Baptist church (24,000-member *Sŏngnak* Church) and the largest Presbyterian congregation (60,000-member Yŏngnak Presbyterian Church).

Korea began to be held up by Christians around the world as an example of how the church really can grow fast. So it came as a shock to many evangelicals when the atmosphere changed and they were suddenly being viewed as problematic and suspicious. They simply weren't accustomed to being seen as part of the problem rather than one of the solutions. Jongho Kim, the former General Secretary of the South Korean student movement InterVarsity Fellowship (IVF), described it to me as being like a chill coming over the work of the church in South Korea. The stratospheric growth of the church came to a screeching halt as fewer people came to outreach events, fewer Koreans were being baptized, and – before long – new students were silently holding up signs so they could avoid even exchanging words with their evangelical classmates. Many observers began describing the Korean church as 'in decline'.[180]

The crisis of trust in the church also hit finances, and giving plummeted in many churches. For IVF, supporting

---

179 Lowman, *The Day of His Power*, p.164.

180 Just type the words 'Korean church in decline' into your browser for a range of articles from well-known publications and news sources.

work on over 160 campuses and funding over 150 full time staff, the last thing they needed was a financial downturn. If anything, now was the time to advance, certainly not to downsize. But events outside their control had struck and moving forward would take something remarkable.

THE TROUBLE WITH SUCCESS

Far away from Korea, a few years before events at that university, a very different kind of financial crisis was brewing. This one was born from success rather than adversity: nobody in Burkina Faso is flashing 'No Thanks' signs at evangelicals. If anything there is more of an atmosphere of 'Yes Please' wherever Jesus is shared. The national student movement, Union des Groupes Bibliques du Burkina Faso (UGBB), had been growing constantly since its foundation almost fifty years previously.[181] They were therefore thrown off-balance by the news that they were about to lose almost all their funding in a single day.

Burkina Faso's capital, Ouagadougou, has maybe my favourite name of any city I have ever visited. It's difficult for an Englishman like me even to pronounce it without sounding at least a little like a Francophone African – try it for yourself! The UGBB office is nestled on an Ouagadougou back street, just across from the main entrance to the university and two doors down from one of the city's most popular student eateries. Goats mingle on the red and dusty streets outside. A tall concrete mosque towers up behind the office courtyard and the call to prayer can often be heard wafting in the background during UGBB staff and student times of prayer.

---

181 The first UGBB cell groups were founded in 1972.

These Arabic intonations, mingling with the passionate intercessions – in French and other languages – of the UGBB community, serve as a constant reminder of the great and unexpected liberty which Christians experience in this Muslim-majority nation. Christians and Muslims, for the most part, manage to coexist comfortably and to speak respectfully of one another's religious convictions. Tensions have flared a little in recent years but these remain the exception. It's no wonder that several Burkinabe Christians told me how – despite its many challenges – they consider their country to be a blessed nation.

I didn't really need much convincing, though, that God is doing amazing things in Burkina Faso. I have rarely witnessed such a sandstorm of outreach activity as I did during my first few hours at the UGBB office. My plan, on arriving in Ouagadougou, had been to hang out at the UGBB office, and from there, visit events and meet both staff and students. I arrived at the airport with a 160-page blank notebook given to me by my mother. It had a Moomin on the front – thanks, Mum! – but, despite the cover's lack of journalistic gravitas, I packed it because I wanted something big enough to record every single detail of what I observed.

It only took until 4pm on my first day for the notebook to contain thirty pages of detailed observations. Not long thereafter it was back in my bag, my ambition to document everything torn to shreds by the sheer volume of action occurring around me: students were gathering for prayer, there were English clubs for outreach, Bible discussions for seekers, mission classes for students who might plant new groups in other cities when they graduate, singing practice for upcoming outreach concerts, and so much else beside.

Sometimes, up to ten events were occurring simultaneously in locations around the city and across the campus. All this on a single day in just one of the thirteen national administrative regions around which UGBB is structured.

Nationwide, thousands of people hear about Jesus each month through UGBB's work. It has all happened, amazingly, with very little outside input. A couple of people vaguely remember a white missionary called Alan, who occasionally travelled in from Ivory Coast to offer advice some decades previously. Another recalled a man from nearby Chad who once lived there for five years. But the stories they told of their movement were mainly of God working through and among the Burkinabe people. They have even become a missionary-sending nation, with UGBB commissioning graduates to serve for various terms in neighbouring nations such as Mali and Guinea, as well as among the many unreached people groups within their own borders.

When Moustapha Ouédraogo, one of the UGBB staff members, took me on a tour of the National Museum, we wandered around examining some strikingly beautiful and ornately carved wooden animal masks used in animistic tribal rituals. A dark wooden antelope head, the length of its curling horns etched with white painted lines and its snout decorated with a series of interlocking triangles, sat across from a giant fish head of similar material and hue whose cavernous interior is designed to fit snugly over a human cranium during ceremonial dances. Yet these gods are increasingly close to becoming mere exhibition pieces, marginalized by the spread of Christian (and Muslim) monotheism. In the past fifty years the number of Burkinabe evangelicals has exploded from 10,000 to well over a million.

It is for this, among other reasons, that the IFES Regional Secretary for Francophone Africa decided in 2004 that UGBB was ready to stand on its own feet and 'graduate' from dependence on outside funding. Until that day their national structures had relied primarily on foreign money being channelled into them by IFES. It was an economic strategy that made sense in this West African nation where the average income hovered around $5 a day.[182] But that was about to change: when I asked Dokassa Combary, UGBB's current Officer of Financial Mobilization, how gradually they were eased away from foreign funding, she laughed and did a sweeping horizontal hand movement followed by a dramatic downwards plunge. There was, she explained, no smooth transition period; they were facing a financial cliff edge. The Regional Secretary's move honoured and dignified what was happening in Burkina Faso but it also threw the staff and board members into shock and uncertainty.

One of the most challenging issues for UGBB was that there is no history in Burkina Faso of local Christians funding anything other than the local church. Faith-based NGOs, like Compassion, are financed entirely from outside the country. It would take a shift of mindset even to have Burkinabe Christians consider making a donation. It would require something even more incredible to fund the student movement in a nation where those few who do have healthy pay cheques often commit much of their extra income to supporting less-fortunate relatives and friends. There's just not much spare cash floating around.

---

182 As reported by various sources. See, for example: 'Burkina Faso MPs agree to cut pay by half', BBC News, 13 January 2015, https://www.bbc.com/news/world-africa-30794822 (Accessed 28 March 2019).

THE CHAPTER I NEARLY DIDN'T WRITE

Money plays a part in every student movement. Staff need to be paid, websites launched, conferences and camps hosted. None of this stuff is free. Yet, for most of us involved in campus ministry, money often seems barely more than an inconvenient necessity – something to which we reluctantly give attention just so everything else can function. Not many people's eyes light up at the words, 'You need to fundraise'. I know mine don't.

As I worked on this book, in fact, I frequently considered removing or replacing this chapter. Everything else I write about is so obviously describing some core aspect of work among students – justice, evangelism, leadership development, engaging our context – but money seemed only mildly more exciting a topic than how to organize your filing cabinet or arrange the furniture in your office. These things matter, of course, but do such administrative details really merit a chapter of equal length to those on proclaiming Jesus and inviting others to follow him?

The problem is that economic themes run right through the gospel narratives of Jesus' life. He bled and died on the cross, in part, as a result of financial factors. Judas sold him for a bag of precious metal. Soldiers, on the payroll of Caesar were – like so many perpetrators of injustice today and throughout history – simply getting their hours in at the office when they hammered metal spikes through his wrists or hands. The crucifixion is a story of how the mightiest financial institution of the day, the Roman Empire, sponsored the torture of God incarnate. And, as a perk of the job, his killers got to take seemingly the only object he owned – his robe – and use it as a fancy poker chip in a spot of workplace recreation.[183]

---

183 Matthew 27:35.

Local religious leaders, who agitated to have him killed, were also motivated partly by economic factors. Jesus spent the week before his death verbally eviscerating them for the way they influenced the nation. He repeatedly told them that their use of material wealth betrayed disdain for everybody but themselves: they wouldn't pay the cost, in time or cash, to feed the hungry or visit the imprisoned.[184] They loved their fancy threads – or 'flowing robes'[185] – and wandered dashingly around the temple making a show of their lavish gifts, which in reality only represented a tiny fraction of their income.[186] They had an Excel spreadsheet which helped them tithe everything, even the herbs in their kitchens, but they allowed their technical exactitude in charitable giving to excuse them from seeking to create a just and merciful nation.[187] They had more reverence for the gold furnishings of the temple, he told them, than for the God to whom the temple was dedicated.[188] There were only so many of these attacks they could take before they dug into their cash reserves, which they refused to use for things like feeding the hungry or providing medical care for the poor, and paid off Judas to help them shut Jesus' mouth forever.[189]

Jesus, in these criticisms, was not simply using financially-themed illustrations to make some higher spiritual point. He seemed instead to be portraying what people do with their wallets as a barometer of their relationship with God. Jesus pinpoints the problem with the Jewish leaders quite

184 Matthew 25:35-45.
185 Luke 20:46.
186 Mark 12:38–39.
187 Matthew 23:23–24.
188 Matthew 23:16–22.
189 Matthew 26:14–16.

precisely in a story which all three synoptic gospels – Matthew, Mark and Luke – identify as the trigger for their plot to have him arrested: the tale of some farmers who rent a vineyard from its owner and who then, when the landlord sends a series of emissaries to request some of the grapes, go on to beat three of these messengers up and eventually kill the fourth, the son of the vineyard owner.[190] The owner responds by having them evicted and executed. In the context, where 'vineyard' was a common symbol for Israel, Jesus' message is clear: they have treated the gifts of God – such as land, nation and temple – as something to be used for their own ends and forgotten to whom it all ultimately belongs. Soon they will lose them all.[191]

Consider Jesus' underlying critique: how, according to his story, did the vineyard tenants get into this mess? By believing that they owned the grape farm and weren't simply looking after it for another. How, by implication, had the Jewish leaders of Jesus' time gone wrong? By treating their nation, land and temple as items they could manipulate for their own benefit rather than as something they were looking after on God's behalf. It was their desire to own and control for themselves, rather than steward and manage on their maker's behalf, from which all the problems stemmed. This despite their own Scriptures – which are also ours – opening with a clear statement that humanity was put into existence to take care of the planet for its creator.[192] They treated their finances like

---

190 Mark 12:1–12, Matthew 21:33–46, Luke 20:9–19.

191 A prophecy which came true during the siege and destruction of Jerusalem in AD 70.

192 Genesis 1:26–30 – a passage often misused as a pretext to exploit and abuse creation, an interpretation which doesn't stand up to much scrutiny when read with care. Also, Genesis 2:15.

they treated their nation and everything else around them –
even the body of God-made-man – as something with which
they could do whatever they liked. The contrast with Jesus,
willingly expending the ultimate resource, himself, on behalf
of them and all of us who have hated and rebelled against our
creator, could not be more stark.

When Jesus ascended, a short while later, he left no
secret bank accounts. His financial plan for the church's
growth seems to have been simply this: that they follow his
teaching and example by generously holding all they had
with open hands and view themselves as stewards rather
than ultimate owners. That neither money, opportunity,
power nor influence be something wielded as if it were their
own, rather than things temporarily entrusted to them for
the service of his kingdom. And this seems to have been
precisely what occurred. Not long after the ascension we
read that the community of believers 'had everything in
common. They sold property and possessions to give to
anyone who had need'.[193] Whilst this doesn't seem to have
survived long as the church's economic system, it did endure
in spirit, with profligacy pervading some churches to the
point that they are described as practising 'rich generosity'
despite 'their extreme poverty', and as giving 'beyond their
ability' to help other believers affected by famine.[194]

Yet, even in this area, the ancient communities of Jesus'
early followers were as patchy in their obedience as they
were in most others. It's striking that the first recorded
internal crisis of the early church after Pentecost was not
doctrinal. It instead revolved around financial ethics. Two

193 Acts 2:44–45.
194 2 Corinthians 8:2–3.

members of the fledgling Jesus community, Ananias and Sapphira, pretended to be more generous than was really the case.[195] When Peter confronted them on the matter they fell dead before him. The next internal tension emerged when widows from one cultural group within the church were receiving less food than another and so the apostles had the church select from among themselves a team of competent administrators to manage their widow-support program.[196] The issue, again, was one of resource management.

These stories aren't there by accident and it's therefore hard to escape the fact that money was not, for Jesus or his early followers, an unfortunate administrative detail. Right financial practice seems to have been at the heart of what it meant to be a community following Jesus. Some of their most unsettling moments, from Judas' betrayal through to the early chapters of Acts, come from not dealing with it well. 'How are you handling money?' seems to have been at least as important a question for the early Christians as 'How's your prayer life?'

Henri Nouwen, in his fascinating little book *A Spirituality of Fundraising*, observes that Christians tend to overlook basic scriptural teaching when developing the financial side of their work: fundraising, according to Nouwen, is giving other people the opportunity to steward their money well – it is a way of helping disciple them in the area of finances by providing an opportunity to reinvest their God-given resources. Having to talk publically about money, he says, also forces the fundraiser to assess their own attitude to this area: 'We will never', he writes, 'be able to ask for money if we

---

195 Acts 5:1–11.
196 Acts 6:1–7.

do not know how we ourselves relate to money'.[197] To raise support, then, is a means for everyone involved to grow in their application of Jesus' teachings to the material world.

SIMILAR BUT DIFFERENT

The biblical principles, then, may be clear. But is it possible to discern any trans-contextual unifying principles in terms of actual strategy? The 160 nations within IFES are all so diverse. You'd struggle to find, for example, two nations more different than Burkina Faso and South Korea. A visit to either's capital city highlights the contrast. Walking along the streets of Ouagadougou, for example, is an exercise in animal-spotting. Goats, chickens and cows meander through the side streets with casual disregard for anyone wanting to squeeze past. The main roads are peppered with stalls selling mango, papaya and avocado, among other locally-grown fruits and vegetables. Over ninety per cent of the population works in agriculture[198] and many Burkinabe have told me that the 'real Burkina Faso' is out in the countryside.

Weaving around the animals is an endless stream of motorcycles. Almost everybody, from students to businesspeople, owns at least one. One Burkinabe student told me that poverty, in Ouagadougou, is merely owning a pedal bike. Material comfort is having a car. But the busyness of any restaurant or shop can be accurately measured by how many motorcycles are lined up outside. Most students, when they have to go back to their homes hundreds of miles

197 Henri Nouwen, *A Spirituality of Fundraising* (Upper Room Books, 2010), p.26.

198 United Nations, 'Food and Agriculture Policy Decision Analysis: Burkina Faso', April 2014, http://www.fao.org/docrep/field/009/i3760e/i3760e.pdf (Accessed 28 March 2019).

away from Ouagadougou, will make the entire journey on their motorcycle, or on the back of someone else's.

Buildings in Ouagadougou generally consist of just one or two storeys. They would be dwarfed by the glass and steel skyscrapers of Seoul. Most of life in the South Korean capital happens above street level in the offices and apartments. There are over one hundred buildings which exceed 180 metres in height – a figure which represents two Statues of Liberty stacked on top of each other. Seoul's tallest structure, the elegant lantern-shaped Lotte World Tower, is topped by a restaurant on its 123rd floor which permits views across the metropolis. The city even has a botanical garden, Skygarden, where over 24,000 flowers, plants and trees hang above the streets and houses.[199] Seoul is literally a city in the clouds. When South Koreans are not in the sky, they are often found under the ground. Around 200 miles of train track run under the city and millions of people ride it to and from work in Seoul each day. Heat and cold are therefore more easily ignored by locals as they move between various climate-controlled settings.

Unlike the Burkinabe, most South Koreans live far from the means of food production. Just six per cent of South Koreans work in agriculture.[200] Animals are, unlike in Ouagadougou, rarely still alive by the time they arrive in the shops. Food is bought pre-packed in supermarkets or sometimes from the city's numerous open markets, the oldest of which dates from the 1400s. Most people work in manufacturing, technology

---

[199] See: Jeanine Barone, 'How Seoul Transformed a Disused Highway Overpass into Botanical Garden in the Sky', *Independent*, 15 May 2018, https://www.independent.co.uk/travel/asia/seoul-skygarden-location-opening-seoullo-7017-south-korea-best-parks-a8346771.html (Accessed 28 March 2019).

[200] United Nations, 'Republic of Korea', http://www.fao.org/nr/water/aquastat/countries_regions/KOR/KOR-CP_eng.pdf (Accessed 28 March 2019).

or services. Brands like Samsung, Hyundai, Kia and LG all have their headquarters in Seoul.

Agrarian vs. industrialized. Local vs. globalized. On the ground vs. in the sky. The contrasts are many. Economists rank South Korea as the twelfth strongest economy in the world.[201] Burkina Faso is number 129 on the same list.[202] As I began to research student ministry in these two countries, I anticipated writing a chapter about the very different ways each movement wrestles with its unique circumstances. I assumed that, considering their numerous differences, there would be limited overlap in how they approach financial sustainability.

What surprised me, though, was to discover that – for all their dissimilarities – both UGBB and IVF have found exactly the same solution for sustaining themselves financially through challenging times. It is an approach which seems to be adopted by almost every durable student movement. So resilient is it that, when I asked Jongho Kim how badly the crisis in Korean evangelicalism had affected their budget, he simply smiled and told me with great satisfaction, 'It didn't hurt us at all.'

JONGHO'S SECRET

Campus ministry costs money. There are ways to be frugal, of course, but nothing written about in the previous chapters of this book came entirely without cost. Room rentals and physical resources, not to mention staff to train and disciple, helped make the Festival of Art in Guatemala a possibility. The UCCF staff worker, Esther in the UK, and Vinoth in Sri

201 World Bank, 'Gross Domestic Product 2017', https://databank.worldbank. org/data/download/GDP.pdf (Accessed 28 March 2019).
202 World Bank, 'Gross Domestic Product 2017' (Accessed 28 March 2019).

Lanka during the civil war, both required salaries in order to devote their time to growing the movement. The many new converts in Mongolia first encountered the message of Jesus in apartments or offices rented by FCS. The list could go on – almost everything costs money. Even just a seminar handout incurs printing costs. It is therefore quite reasonable that both UGBB and IVF were worried when their income stream was threatened.

When Jongho told me that the crisis in South Korea had left their movement unscathed, I raised my eyebrows in surprise and asked, 'How so?' I was intrigued as to how they might have ridden out this storm. He replied simply, 'We are supported by our graduates.' He went on to explain that many decades of carefully cultivating a network of former students who follow and invest in the movement's ongoing work – not to mention a solid history of transparency, integrity and good stewardship in financial dealings – meant that even when many Korean Christians were losing confidence in the leadership of the wider church, they still felt attached and enthusiastic enough to give to the work of the student movement. UGBB, who are only just beginning their journey towards financial sustainability, have discovered the same thing. It is those who have experienced and benefitted from their ministry who are most likely to invest in its future.

What Jongho was describing is team-based funding. It's one of four main ways to finance a Christian ministry. The full list includes:

1. Commercial transactions: selling items or services in order to generate income for the ministry.
2. Grant-based funding: obtaining money from charitable trusts which exist to distribute funds to good causes.

3. Capital campaigns: raising money through one-off donations from a range of people and sources.
4. Team-based: having a range of givers who involve themselves by making regular, possibly automatic, donations every month, quarter or year.

Each of these approaches has a long history within IFES. Most movements, for example, charge fees for student conferences. IVF and many other student movements also have a publishing arm which produces and sells books. UGBB is working on a plan to open a small printing supplies store. But the profit margins on such ventures are usually small. Student conferences cannot be very expensive or nobody will come. Students are relatively 'penniless' in every nation and many movements subsidize such events. And, with a few exceptions, Christian publishing is rarely the path to great riches. Commercial transactions tend to be, at best, a supplement to a movement's income rather than their economic backbone.

Grant-based funding is also very helpful for certain initiatives. Dieudonné Tindano, the General Secretary of UGBB, told me that they had received some grants for various innovative evangelism projects such as a sports-based outreach and a musical theatre festival. But it is relatively rare for a charitable trust to make grants towards the everyday running costs of a ministry. They tend to give towards specific time-limited projects.

Capital campaigns are also useful for those moments when an unusually swift or large infusion of cash is required. Purchasing a national office or printing gospels for a large outreach are two common examples. But dependence on one-off donations for ongoing ministry costs such as salaries is exhausting. It requires constantly chasing and requesting support from a range of sources. Such work is sustainable for a short period but can swiftly become counter-productive as many supporters develop a sense that you are only interested in their cash.

Healthy sustainable ministry usually requires a custom blend of commerce, grant-based funding and capital campaigns. But the simplest and most maintainable method of financing a student movement's regular costs is cultivating a network of former students – along with other interested people and churches – who follow and invest in its ongoing work. In other words: team-based funding. This will include requests for money. But once a person is involved through giving then the work becomes much simpler: one simply needs to keep them informed of what is happening – they need to remain conscious of what they are supporting and why. Unlike with capital campaigns or grant-based funding, the need to constantly go back asking for more is reduced.

STORIES AND SYSTEMS

Successfully building a support team requires a shift in mindset. Kehinde Ojo, IFES Program Director for Indigenous Support Development, told me, 'It is important for us to broaden our concept of "fundraising" to incorporate mobilizing time, talent and treasures.' He argues that our fixation with cash has blinded us to other ways to approach support development. This realization came home to him during a fuel crisis in his homeland of Nigeria. The crisis was not a matter of cash; demand was simply outstripping supply, and most local fuel pumps were empty. Kehinde, then a travelling staff member responsible for supporting groups on several campuses, relied heavily on his car and found himself unable to do his job.

One evening, while visiting a graduate of the movement and sharing stories about life and ministry, he was politely asked what kind of drink he would like in order to refresh himself. Kehinde, knowing that the graduate's spouse worked in an oil firm and so may have safely stored fuel at home in containers, replied 'Petrol, please,' and – to his delight – the graduate agreed to give him four gallons of fuel.

As Kehinde drove away later that evening, in a car full of fuel paid for by a friend, he realized that this was the essence of building a support team: tell others the stories and make it simple for them to give. This was a far cry from his previous understanding of fundraising, which involved constantly communicating budgetary shortfalls and hoping that new people would reach into their pockets to give. He says that instead of going to churches and speaking primarily about their needs, he increasingly spoke of what God was doing – and the vision he had given them for the future – and relegated economic matters to a briefer mention. Kehinde told me that when students and staff ask him what they should do if they have two minutes to share with a group of people, say a church, he always tells them to narrate a recent happening. 'We must,' he said, 'speak of needs in the context of vision.' Financial development, he insists, is as much the task of storytelling as anything else.

What needs to accompany storytelling is accessible systems of giving. At the graduate's house, Kehinde's task was simple: he only had to say, 'Petrol, please!' There was no need for his friend to leap acrobatically through multiple proverbial hoops. He just needed to grab a nearby container and fill the tank. For those of us building a support team, simple giving systems are essential: friends who engage with our stories need a very straightforward path to implementing their interest in becoming financially part of the work. Dieudonné told me, for example, that in Burkina Faso many people connected with their work are not in the habit of wiring money, so UGBB have to make physical visits to receive promised support in cash.[203] But they don't wait for people to come and bring it to them (though some come anyway): the aim is to put the effort of collecting financial investments on the receiving organization rather than the partnering individual, and to make it as easy as possible for the support team to follow through on their good intentions.

UGBB apply the same logic to the way they create online and mobile payment systems for their support team. This is not just for local giving. UGBB also draw on a network of people who can't be reached on foot: the Burkinabe diaspora. Just before I visited Ouagadougou, Dieudonné had taken a tour of the United States and Canada. Ethnic and national groups, in many countries, often disproportionately emigrate to a handful of specific areas. So tens of thousands of Brits end up on the southern and eastern coast of Spain, hundreds of thousands of Cubans live in Miami, Chicago bills itself as the second largest Polish city outside Warsaw, and up to forty per cent of some Los Angeles high schools are first or second generation Iranian.[204] These patterns

---

203 To emphasize: these aren't cold calls – they're ways to collect money already promised.

204 Shoku Amirani, 'Tehrangeles: How Iranians made part of LA their own', *BBC News*, 29 September 2012, https://www.bbc.com/news/magazine-19751370, (Accessed 28 March 2019).

stem from the fact that it's easier to move to where you have friends and family already, as well as the way different settings appeal to the needs and priorities of each group (chilly rain-soaked Brits are drawn to the Spanish sun like moths to a lamp!) alongside other factors like historic colonial, business, trading and educational links between locations. When Dieudonné told me some of the places he'd been in North America, I was surprised by the names; they were not globally-renowned urban centres. But it was there, in places like small-town Oklahoma, that he was able to gather graduates of UGBB, fill them in on the work, and ask them to pray regularly for what was happening.

Kehinde says that, thanks to social media, we live in a golden age for both simple giving systems and means of dispersing narratives among a wide audience. Both UGBB and IVF make full use of the online tools available to them. Most IVF groups have a Facebook page on which streams of photos and snippets from campuses appear so graduates and current students can track their work. The movement also sends out email updates and a physical newsletter, each of them packed full of stories. Dieudonné showed me, on his mobile phone, how he runs several WhatsApp groups for the UGBB graduates, both those at home and also the diaspora groups he contacted and gathered in North America (as well as in Europe), and sends them a regular stream of photos and stories. None of this is exactly rocket science, of course: most of us are accustomed to using such online tools in our daily lives. What makes the difference is when a student movement doesn't see them as playful distractions but as valuable instruments for the storytelling aspect of support development and, as a result, they invest time and energy in thoughtfully and consistently developing their use.

Such tools, however, are not without their drawbacks. Kehinde says that, ideally, a student movement will source the majority of its support locally. One reason is simply the dignity it bestows upon the organization and nation. Around eighty per cent of UGBB's budget is currently met by people based in Burkina Faso, with a further seven per cent coming from the Burkinabe diaspora and the rest from a combination of foreign contacts and a fellow IFES movement in Europe.[205] When I met with their finance team, they said that the shift towards local funding is increasing their sense that God can use each of them in every aspect of his work, including the monetary aspect. One of them recalled that a board member exclaimed, when making his first gift to the movement after the withdrawal of central funds from IFES, 'Praise the Lord; I did not know that from my personal salary I could support another person!'

Kehinde says such joy at becoming financially self-sustaining is common. He listed the first four benefits of a primarily local support base as the *sense of fulfilment* this provides to the movement and the indigenously-led church, the *sense of ownership* it grows in the work among graduates and the wider Christian community, its *sustainability* (built, as it is, on maintainable relationships which require limited travel) and the way it *strengthens* the commitment of graduates and friends to the work by involving them in a concrete way.[206]

---

205 Figures supplied to me by Dokassa Combary, UGBB's current Head of Financial Mobilization, and by UGBB General Secretary Dieudonné Tindano. I have used their 2018 figures for this chapter; 79% of their projected 2018 budget was covered (meaning a 21% shortfall) with 80% of actual income coming from internal sources, 7% from the diaspora, and 13% from other IFES movements. Each year varies and the 2017 figures were 85% internal, 5% diaspora, and 10% IFES (with a 20% shortfall), while the 2016 numbers were 64% internal, 3% diaspora, and 33% IFES (with a 5% shortfall).

206 A good document on this topic is: IFES, *Indigenous Support Development Training Manual 2017 Edition* (IFES, 2017).

The fifth gain of building a local support team, Kehinde told me, is that it provides accountability. It's easy to send out messages far afield which give an impression that things are going a certain way, when the reality is very different. But when your support team lives nearby, and may, indeed, even have *their* church's students participating in *your* group, well … it's just a little harder to be anything other than authentic. Jongho told me that one of the reasons IVF managed to retain its funding, despite the crisis engulfing the wider Korean church, is not just that they projected an aura of integrity and good stewardship via their newsletters and social media, but also because their graduates could see close up what they were doing and they stuck with the student movement.

Storytelling may become more complicated as we move away from simple conversations with friends. But the principles remain similar: forming connections, communicating what God is doing and making it easy for people to become involved financially as well as in other ways.

BEYOND THE BUDGET

Financial sustainability, then, is more than a matter of getting the budget covered. The way a movement approaches this issue affects its relationship with graduates and local churches. It becomes missionally-transformative when our community sees God supply all we need. Our own sense of dignity and ownership of the work – not to mention confidence in God's sufficiency and power – grow as a result. We see in more than a theoretical sense that *he* can handle this and that he can do so through *us*.

It is, of course, a biblical theme that those with much have an obligation towards those with relatively little. Christians from harder currency nations, with higher-ranking economies, have a role to play in helping financially support the church in other areas of the world. In UGBB, around a quarter of their budget is supplied by friends from outside the country, though – as we saw – the overwhelming majority now comes from Burkinabe believers. It's a nice combination of a local core with an international supplement. Whether our support comes from near or far, though, the goal of financial sustainability is inseparable from the task of storytelling. Even in a nation where 'no thanks' signs are being flashed, the work can continue if we have a team of partners who are aware of what God is doing through us and who are willing to say 'Yes please' to being a part of it through their prayers and also through their physical resources.

QUESTIONS FOR REFLECTION OR DISCUSSION:

How do you feel about the financial aspect of Christian mission on campus? Does it excite you, scare you, does it hold no interest for you or something else? Why do you think this is?

Looking at your own attitude to money, do you tend to see yourself more as an owner or a steward? How does this play out in practice?

Have you ever thought that you might be part of God's plan for financing and resourcing his mission? How might this look for you personally?

How well does your group or movement tell the story of what God is doing among them to those who do (or could) partner financially with your mission? What practical ways could you/they develop in this area?

CONCLUSION: THE UNREACHED ISLAND

STORIES FROM THE FUTURE (ST KITTS)

Slipping slowly from the edge of the bed my socks gently brush against the floor. My daughter's face scrunches in her sleep as she murmurs. I pause and wait to see what will happen. She rolls onto her side and becomes still again, her little torso rising and falling almost imperceptibly with every sleeping breath. After waiting for a few more moments, I very slowly creep across the darkened room, the vertical line of dull light emanating from the doorway – the door is slightly ajar – providing me with my direction, and eventually I am able to reach the handle. Pulling it towards me, I open it just enough to avoid illuminating her face, and slide snugly through it. I turn and gently close the door behind me (the click of it closing can sometimes jolt her awake). Today, though, she makes no response.

Walking into the adjoining room I see my children's Bible sitting on the sofa. Most nights we try to read from it and then all pray together before bed. My kids are small – Jackson is eight, William is six and Amélie is four – and we want them to know the joy of following Jesus from a young age. Every night, in fact, we pray that each of us will love him for all of our long healthy lives, and know how much he loves us. Over the years that follow I know that their personal stories will take a variety of twists and turns, but – as I pick up and close the Bible, slotting it onto a nearby shelf beside the picture book *Here Come Ducklings* – I again pray for them to know him.

Moving from the living room I head across the hallway to my bedroom where my laptop is sitting on a black IKEA desk. To one side is a pile of papers with notes from interviews and visits undertaken for *Campus Lights*. Tonight I will be adding to their number: I am concluding the research portion of the book by talking with Tonia Hemmings-White on the Caribbean island of St Kitts. We've been playing communicatory ping-pong through email and WhatsApp for over a week, attempting somehow to match up our schedules for this conversation. The previous night some time zone confusion, arising from a six-hour difference, meant we missed one another. It's been a recurring theme in my research, as several people featured in previous chapters can attest. Today, though, things work out – she answers when I dial at the arranged moment.

Tonia moved to St Kitts fourteen months previously. Her husband, a pharmacist, got a job there, and she now combines her time between staying at home with their two children – aged seven and two – and also doing a spot of freelance work as a relief pharmacist. The couple are originally from Jamaica and Tonia credits her critical formation as a follower of Jesus to her years of participation in the IFES-linked high school movement there. The work in Jamaica is some of the oldest in the world. It was founded after an unexpected stopover on the island in 1944 inspired IFES General Secretary Stacey Woods to send them, in 1948, Canadian staff worker Cathie Nicholl who would spend three months putting the movement on its feet.[207] From there, under local leadership, it spread out across the Caribbean region, with Jamaican IVCF (since renamed UCCF) graduates initiating work in Trinidad and Guyana, and former students from the new movements in those countries going on to pioneer work in other neighbouring nations.[208]

When Tonia moved to St Kitts, she had no intention of becoming the next Cathie Nicholl. But a year after arriving, she received a text message from a Jamaican friend asking her if she'd be willing to show IFES Caribbean Regional Secretary Desmond Rogers around the island. He wanted to scout it as a possible location for initiating a new work. St Kitts – despite its relatively small population of around 35,000 people – is home to six different universities and numerous high schools. Desmond wanted to start making contacts and Tonia was happy to be his tour guide.

Tonia says that when Desmond arrived, she had a strange sense that God would speak to her that day. She even told Desmond that she thought God had something to say and that she was waiting to hear it. As they travelled around educational institutions, an interesting phenomenon occurred: people kept pointing at her during conversations and saying, 'You are the one who is leading the work here.' She would always smile and shake her head, and explain that she was just helping out for the day. But as their travels continued, she began to sense that maybe this was from

---

207 In 1948 she started the high schools' ministry. In 1952 she made another short visit to help start the work among tertiary students.

208 Historical sketch courtesy of current and previous Caribbean Regional Secretaries, Desmond Rogers and Marc Pulvar, as well as: Lowman, *The Day of His Power*, pp.291–295.

God. By the time Desmond left, she told him she was happy to continue helping in any way she could.

When we spoke, there was no IFES work in any of the high schools or universities of St Kitts. But Tonia was one month away from the intended launch of lunchtime or after-school groups in several secondary institutions. In a year or so, she hopes to initiate groups in the universities and already has a plan for how to do so. When I asked her about the challenges of her context, she replied that difficulties were not at the forefront of her mind: she just looks at St Kitts and constantly tells herself, 'This place is ripe.' It seems like a place full of young people ready to hear and respond to the message of Jesus. She says she is constantly thinking of Jesus' words, that 'the harvest is plentiful but the workers are few' and we should 'ask the Lord of the harvest … to send out workers'.[209] She prays that the small beginnings of her and Desmond trailing around the island together will lead to teams of students forming across St Kitts to live and speak for Jesus within their institutions and among their colleagues.

When my conversation with Tonia concludes, I finish typing up my notes and thoughts, close the laptop and glance up at an old history of IFES from the 1980s that rests on my bookshelf. It's inspiring to see the ways God is, still now, constantly expanding and renewing this global movement. Getting up from my desk I return to the living room where our family earlier prayed and read a Bible story. I think of my children: will they go to university? Maybe not. There are plenty of other good paths to follow. My middle son is named after one of my grandfathers, whose

---

209 Matthew 9:37–38.

tertiary education was an engineering apprenticeship, while the other's name was borrowed from both my wife's great-grandfather – a lifelong barber in a small town in South Carolina – and also my childhood grandfather figure, a manual labourer. Perhaps they will follow in their namesakes' footsteps.

But if they do go to university (or college or a polytechnic), I hope that there is a community of their colleagues seeking to be the lights of their campus. In their fleeting-but-pivotal student years, I pray that they will be participants in a team which proclaims Jesus, engages the issues of the day, develops leaders and – through all this – is readied for a life partnering with God in his mission wherever they reside and work. I am thankful that, if all goes smoothly for Tonia, there will – in coming years – be several more institutions with such groups.

And so I pray for the constant renewal of those student movements which have existed for many years or even decades, the growth and expansion of the ones just beginning, and for all of us involved at any level of IFES – whether as students, graduates, staff, supporters or simply as interested observers and readers – to remain constant in our prayers for the communities and individuals which live and speak for Jesus on the diverse array of campuses around the world. May his work among students grow and be renewed each year as the Spirit works in and through them. And may we continue to see 'students built into communities of disciples, transformed by the gospel and impacting the university, the church and society for the glory of Christ.'[210]

---

210 Phrase borrowed from IFES' *Living Stones* document, see Appendix Two.

QUESTIONS FOR REFLECTION OR DISCUSSION:

What, from this book, most struck you as relevant for your own context? If you were to do one thing differently as a result of reading it, what would that be?

Has this book affected, confirmed or challenged your understanding or perspective on Christian mission among students? If so, how?

If you had to pick one thing from this book to pray about regularly, what would it be?

APPENDIX ONE: THE IFES DOCTRINAL BASIS

The IFES doctrinal basis shall be the central truths of Christianity, as revealed in Scripture, including:

- The unity of the Father, Son and Holy Spirit in the Godhead.
- The sovereignty of God in creation, revelation, redemption and final judgment.
- The divine inspiration and entire trustworthiness of Holy Scripture, as originally given, and its supreme authority in all matters of faith and conduct.
- The universal sinfulness and guilt of all people since the fall, rendering them subject to God's wrath and condemnation.
- Redemption from the guilt, penalty, dominion and pollution of sin, solely through the sacrificial death (as our representative and substitute) of the Lord Jesus Christ, the incarnate Son of God.
- The bodily resurrection of the Lord Jesus Christ from the dead and his ascension to the right hand of God the Father.
- The presence and power of the Holy Spirit in the work of regeneration.
- The justification of the sinner by the grace of God through faith alone.
- The indwelling and work of the Holy Spirit in the believer.
- The one holy universal Church which is the body of Christ and to which all true believers belong.
- The expectation of the personal return of the Lord Jesus Christ.

APPENDIX TWO:
SUMMARY OF LIVING STONES

Below is a summative excerpt from *Living Stones*, an August 2008 IFES document which clarified the vision of the global movement. *Living Stones* summarizes IFES' vision of 'students built into communities of disciples, transformed by the gospel and impacting the university, the church and society for the glory of Christ'.[211] *Campus Lights* draws its shape from the first section, 'Strategic Priorities', though it touches on some of the others:

STRATEGIC PRIORITIES

To meet our vision of growth and depth of impact, we will focus on six key areas, with one defining path running through all the priorities: to release the creativity and energy of students.

1. Communicating the good news of Jesus Christ
2. Strengthening leadership and *formación*
3. Promoting student-graduate integration
4. Building sustainable support
5. Addressing current global issues
6. Engaging the University

Releasing student initiative

---

211 https://ifesworld.org/en/our-vision.

FIRM FOUNDATIONS

Recognising that strong growth needs firm foundations, we will invest in identifying and initiating excellence and best practice in five critical areas.

1. Governance
2. Organisationl development
3. Global partnerships
4. Human resources and pastoral care
5. Research and innovation

CORE COMMITMENTS

As we work to achieve our vision, every aspect of IFES life will be surrounded and supported by three core commitments.

1. Prayer
2. Scripture engagement
3. Community

ACKNOWLEDGEMENTS

Campus Lights began life five years ago as a sketched outline in my notebook on a Sunday morning. But its origins lie much further back than that. My two decades of involvement in the student world and IFES are thanks to a number of people who helped involve and keep me in the movement over the years. This is probably a good place to give a shout out to those people: Steve and Chris Owens, who actively encouraged my involvement with the Christian Union during my first disorienting months as an undergraduate in 1997 and who involved me in work with international students via their church and through Friends International.

Alison Williams, who was my UCCF staff worker from 1998, and was a sounding board and advisor when I first applied to work for IFES in Romania in 2001 and later in the UK in 2007.

Mike and Kris York, to whom this book is dedicated, and who welcomed me into their home and mission as my team leaders during my first stint in Romania from 2001 to 2004, and who – as well as still being some of my closest collaborators – have also become like family to us and are some of the guests my children are most excited to see come and visit.

My teammates on the UCCF Midlands team and the students I served alongside with the Christian Unions of Keele, Staffordshire University in Stoke and Stafford, Buxton, Harper Adams and MMU Cheshire from 2007 to 2012 – I think you all know which among you was my favourite.[212]

---

212 That's right: it was *your* Christian Union.

Terry Erickson and Sarah Schilling for having me write numerous articles for IVCF between 2011 and 2014.

Lindsay Brown for involving me in FEUER since 2011 and being a mentor to myself and our team as we develop public campus-based outreach in Romania.

Finally, our friends from OSCER with whom we love partnering.

As for turning love of students and a notebook sketch into this book: Tim Adams, from IFES, encouraged this project from the beginning and helped suggest countries and people worth contacting. He also first pointed me towards Muddy Pearl as a possible publisher. Thanks Tim! And thank you also to the good people at Muddy Pearl, especially to Stephanie Heald for being willing to believe in *Campus Lights*, and to Fiona Houston and Healey Roseweir for all your work on it.

I'd also like to give a nod towards Al Hsu, who edited my previous book (with IVP) and first affirmed to me that *Campus Lights* was a timely project and one which might viably also be tied into the 2019 IFES World Assembly – Al, your words helped get the ball rolling on it all.

My immense gratitude also goes to all those who hosted me and took the time to show me around their countries and movements, or agreed to be interviewed by me, correspond with me or provide me with contacts or insights. It's a list that includes, though is not limited to: Adrian, Alex, Andy, Anaeli, Annette, Ariunaa, Arul, Barnabas, Barry, Benita, Blake, Brianna, Caitlin, Cameron, Chinba, Chimka, Chuka, Dalcy, Danny, David B, Debby, Desmond, Deve, Dieudonné, Dileni, Dokassa, Dramane, Dtgoo, Emanuel, Esther, 'Eurasian translator', Faisal, 'Florin', 'Fouad', Greg, Ghaith, George, Godfrey, 'Hazim', Howard, Isabel, Israel,

Iwel, Jean Marie, Jhonny, Joe, Joel, John, Jongho, Joshua, Katie, Kehinde, Kumuthini, Laurenţiu, Lee, Lucian, Marc, Maria, 'Mariam', Martha, Martin, Mary, Maureen, Mercy, Mirek, Moustapha, Naomi, Nomwendé, Nydia, Otto, Oyuka, Patrick, Paul, 'Pepper', Priyan, Ruth S, Ruth R, Saikhanaa, Saji, Salim, Seiza, Shagai, Shantanu, Steve, Sunder Singh, Sung Woo, Susan, Teddy, Thurston, Timothée, Tim A, Tim R, Tom, Tommy, Tonia, Tsoog, Tumee, Unuruu, Vinicio, Vineshka, Vinoth, Yohan, Yuka, and Zulaa. Not all of you were directly cited but you each helped shape the book. My especial thanks to those of you who took the time to read and correct what I had written for accuracy; I greatly appreciate you doing so.

Thank you to those friends and others who took the time to read and give feedback on either the entire manuscript or specific chapters during the initial writing period; Lucian Bălănescu, Whitney Cawley, Priyan Dias, Greg Jao, Timothée Joset, Kristi Mair, Kehinde Ojo, Caitlin Ormiston and Deve Tampubolon. Your input was invaluable! Kristi and Caitlin have also been an extra help as constant sounding boards on the conceptual development of this book.

Shin Maeng, thank you for the beautiful piece of art you created for the cover, which really brings to life the substance of *Campus Lights* in a fresh and eye-catching manner.

Thank you also to my Mum, whose suggestion – combined with some thoughts from Alex Damian – led to the idea of calling this book *Campus Lights*.

My freedom to write, speak and pursue the things to which God has called me is made possible by those friends who involve themselves in the work of Chrysolis through their prayers and financial giving. Thank you so much for enabling me to keep investing my life in this way. My especial thanks here go to the board of trustees for Chrysolis, who are such a tremendous support – Caitlin, Hannah Giddings, Kristi, Stephen Humphreys and Trevor Raaff.

My thanks to our little team in Bucharest – Lucian, Emi Ologeanu and Anca Necula – for your patience as the latter stages of research and writing temporarily absorbed my focus; I am excited about what God has done and is doing through us and around us.

My wife Whitney; 'the girl from English camp'. I am thankful for your beauty, kindness, wit, intelligence and passion, for how deeply you love me and our children and for your constant desire to thoughtfully apply to all of life your love for Jesus, driven by your sense of how much he loves you and others in our world. I am also appreciative of the space you made for me to write this book. In the midst of what was possibly our most crazily-packed year yet, you bore much of the workload as I travelled and wrote.

My children, Jackson, William and Amélie: I am thankful to have been gifted you and pray that you grow in your love and knowledge of Jesus. I know that you will ask me 'did you mention me in your book?', so here is one of the two places you'll find your names!

And most of all, thank you to our Father who brings us into his work and chooses to use each of us in ways both undeserved and unexpected! *Slavă Domnului!*[213]

---

213 Thank God!